Young Writers

Spellbound

Coventry

Poetry Now
Young Writers

Edited by Sarah Andrew

First published in Great Britain in 1998 by
POETRY NOW YOUNG WRITERS
1-2 Wainman Road, Woodston,
Peterborough, PE2 7BU
Telephone (01733) 230748

HB ISBN 1 86188 880 5
SB ISBN 1 86188 885 6

FOREWORD

In this, our 5th competition year, we are proud to present *Spellbound Coventry.* This anthology represents the very best endeavours of the children from this region.

The standard of entries was high, which made the task of editing a difficult one, but nonetheless enjoyable. The variety of subject matter, creativity and imagination never ceases to amaze and is indeed an inspiration to us all.

This year's competition attracted the highest entry ever - over 46,000 from all over the UK, and for the first time included entries from English speaking children living abroad.

Congratulations to all the writers published in *Spellbound Coventry.* We hope you enjoy reading the poems and that your success will inspire you to continue writing in the future.

Contents

THE POEMS

The Earth Of The Galaxy

Before the beginning of time
And before the mighty ancient civilisations,
There were microscopic molecules scattered
Through countless distances.
Suddenly the molecules collided
And this glorious chemical reaction happened
That made the miracle of life.
The heavens were finally created,
The sun started flowing with its energetic ray
Of pure light, so radiant.
All the mammals, birds, reptiles
And amphibians lived together
In perfect harmony - no destruction at all.

Lee Birta (12)
Ash Green School

Scared

My heart was pounding
Tears were running down my face
I was sweating really bad
I started to run
My blood went cold
I was shivering
My fingers went numb
At last I was home
And I wasn't scared anymore.

Mark Druse (11)
Ash Green School

Never Give In

Your eyes are like the flowers in May
As is the perfume that you wear.
Your hair is like a winter's day
But I do not mean to stare.

I love the way you walk into a room
And I really do admire you.
I hope our love will one day bloom
Because I'd be lost without you.

I remember the day you refused me
Because I went home sad.
That day you really hurt me
Yet that's why I'm glad.

Because it showed me I couldn't always win
And also - never, ever to give in.

John Flowers (15)
Ash Green School

The Battle

It's dark and mysterious
Fierce and frightening
Fighting ferociously, slashing scraping
The warriors are focused
Teeth gritted and eyes alert
Loud and angrily they swing their swords
They're like animals.

Aaron Blackwell (14)
Ash Green School

Man Eater

Ferocious monster
Mouth of knives
Down his throat
The victims slide

Snake-like dragon
Scales of death
Inside screaming people
Struggling for breath.

Loved ones looking
Searching for the lost
On the ground
His slithering mark is embossed.

This deadly serpent
Mysterious yet strong
After its meal
It roars its lonely song.

Away in the darkness.
It slides through the night
To its home where it sleeps,
Under stars shining bright.

Gemma Worwood (14)
Ash Green School

Cats

My cat is coloured black and white
But he only goes out at night
Once it had a very big fright
And that was the last we saw of
him on that cold black night.

Chris Henton (13)
Ash Green School

The Face

A dull plain face
Stone-cold like ice
High up on a wall
Overlooking the land that was a kingdom.
Eyes like stone
Glaring at you
Fixed on a battlement
Overlooking the land that was his kingdom.
Chipped and old
A crown like gold
Gold as the morning sun
Overlooking the land that was the kingdom.

Richard Nailor (14)
Ash Green School

War

Now the war is over
The fields are dead and bare

The memories of all the blood and tears are too much to bear

I see all the horror of war as I walk through a town destroyed

All my family are dead and I only have happy memories to comfort me

I don't know why war has to happen?

It would stop all the tears and discomfort if they thought of another way to sort out their problems.

Lisa Rawlings (13)
Ash Green School

The Golden Bowl

My bowl is gold and is made for a king
In its reflection you can see everything
It reminds me of a precious ancient relic
In its detail it looks all angelic.

I would really love to treasure this bowl
But it might belong to another soul
It looks perfect with a tint in the light
When you get close it's a beautiful sight

The air is still and there is not a sound
I love this sense of peace I have found
My bowl is gold and is made for a king
In its reflection you imagine everything.

Paul Greasley (14)
Ash Green School

The Graveyard

I look at the scary shadows lurking in the mist
as the sound of leaves crumple on the pavement.
I hear a startled scream
and sense the shadows of people lurking around.
Footsteps come towards me they get louder and louder.
I can hear a shadow calling me
I feel something on my shoulder as a chill
goes up my spine.
The shadow shouts 'Help' in an icy way
which scares me even more I feel I have to get
away.

Leanne Ridd (13)
Ash Green School

Barney, Memories

Barney was a fireside dog,
he would sit all day and
let the heat absorb into his
golden coat.

He was a foot-stool to
rest your feet on whilst
watching TV.

He would lie on his
bean-bag and blow bubbles,
while staring at you
to get him his tea.

Barney bubble the
fireside dog will live
with me forever.

Samantha Bole (13)
Ash Green School

Horror

H orrible slimy, creepy things.
O ribble rats, flies and bats.
R inging their web around your head.
R eady to catch their prey and then
they can rest for the day.
O ver windowsills they crawl.
R eady to snap, and snarl and drawl.

Amy Bullock & Claire Neale (13)
Ash Green School

THE CLOUD

The cloud,
Flying high,
Watching the world below.
The cloud,
Putting on its best fluff,
To show the world what life
Is about.
The cloud,
Flying high,
Watching the world below.
The cloud,
Seeing the bad side of life.
Pollution, deaths and wars.
The cloud,
Flying high,
Watching the world below.

Lindsey Willshee (12)
Ash Green School

EXPRESSIONS

The room is dark
their faces are pale.
The atomosphere's sad
and the air smells stale.
One prays for something
another looks on.
There's concern all around
what's lost has now been found.

Colin Bell (14)
Ash Green School

Racism

Colour is used in everything
But when it comes down to skin, it's another thing
Everyone is equal and the same
Just remember, racism is not a game
It doesn't really matter if you're black or white
If everyone works together, it can be alright
People make a judgement of you from the colour of
your skin.
It's not what's on the outside that counts, it's what
there is within.
If it was you, it would be a different matter
Racism will be here next year and the year after
If everyone works together in harmony
The world can be right for you and me.

Harleen Hayer (12)
Ash Green School

The Screaming Death

A reptile sliding on uneven ground.
Worming through your brain
Not making a sound.
Riding across your subconscious minds.
Twisting your dreams inside out.
Turning life upside down.
Screaming for you, to release him.
Now releasing him upon you.
Its hypnotic powers.
A prolonged derangement.
Of unequal prowess.

Lawrence Bound (11)
Ash Green School

The Man On The Street

I feel sorry for the man on the street,
with no friends or family
there are not many people who care.

I feel sorry for the man on the street,
With no one to love
apart from him and the cold air.

I feel sorry for the man on the street,
with straggly clothes
and straggly hair.

I feel sorry for the man on the street,
with no money, he has to beg to get food,
most people must think he's a tramp,
I feel sorry for him, he must have feelings,
hope and a heart.
So next time when you see a man on the street
don't say anything,
Just think if you were there, instead of him.

Kimberley Sey (11)
Ash Green School

Magic

Whistling and flowing
Like water from a mountain
Transparent fire, screams through the air
It whistles and wanders and screams through the night
It burns through the trees but no harm is really done.
As the fire and air and the colours of night,
Explode into the most colourful light you could ever imagine
For this is the power of magic.

Luke Smith (12)
Ash Green School

All Alone

It's all dark, there's a full moon.
I wish my parents would come home soon.
Rustling branches, make me quiver
It's got so cold, I start to shiver
The wind sounds like voices in my head
But it's just fear, I've been misled.
Out of the window, I saw a man in black
With something weird upon his back
As he went passed the window he lifted his head
It looked like he had come back from the dead.
What if he saw me
And started running towards me?
Would I shout and scream?
I wish that this was all a dream
Suddenly there was a knock at the door.
Should I answer it, or just ignore?
It could be him but I was not sure
I walked slowly up to the door
With shaky fingers I opened the door
I had never been so scared before.
But there in front of me I could now see
My parents standing before me.

Stacey Foster (13)
Ash Green School

Autumn

A utumn leaves, the trees so bare,
U nder trees, the leaves lie there.
T all and big, the trees stay there.
U pon the ground, the leaves gather round.
M ore and more leaves upon the ground.
N ow the leaves are there alone.

Adam Hancock (11)
Ash Green School

LIFE

There's so much to life,
But little we know.
There's genes and genetics,
Folk and foe.
There's people, relationships, babies too
All that we live for and all that we do.

Our life's full of things,
Different to some.
Drugs, drink and driving,
Are they to blame
Some people say they have only had one
Have they no shame?
But that's one less life for someone to live.

So understand laws,
Don't drink and drive
Don't take drugs
Live a normal happy life.

Ruth Renshaw (13)
Ash Green School

THE CHINESE HORSE

Blue and green against a black background,
It has a nice jumping sensation,
Like Black Beauty on TV
It's smooth and dull,
Quiet and still,
A jade horse with a scary face,
Making a leap for freedom.

Lee Whetston (14)
Ash Green School

The Door Of My Life

As I open the door and start walking,
I find myself travelling through the rainforest of 7CS.
I step over the green coloured marsh
and get tangled in the big tropical leaves.
I then step over the great brown log.
I can hear laughter, knowing I'm near the end.
I see a stream of light and run towards it.
I step onto the cold, hard, grey floor.
I look around, I see people running out of the door.
I follow them down a flight of windy stairs
And out of a pair of double doors.
Into the cold winter's air onto a big playground.
There's shouting - 'It's not fair! Give it back.'
And chanting - 'One, two, three.'
A bell rings
and there's silence everywhere.

Hayley O'Donnell (12)
Ash Green School

Scared

I was singing a song and I kept hearing a noise.
The noise came from the corner of the room.
All what was in the corner, was my figure doll.
The doll was a clown, from my nan years ago.
The sound was a very evil laugh,
It sounded like someone who was daft.
At first I thought it was a bear,
Which made me even more scared.
But all that while it was that clown doll,
From my nan, long ago.

Nikita Flanaghan (11)
Ash Green School

THE FOUR SEASONS

In winter the snow will fall,
The wind will blow hard and strong.
Winter is a time for snowmen,
Children throwing snowballs,
In the white snow, covering the street.

In spring the flowers bloom,
And baby animals are born.
Baby lambs, baby calves and lots more too.
Spring is a time for sun and rain,
And joy and happiness.

In summer the sun will shine,
Cold drinks and holidays come to mind,
Sun, sand and sea and watching the blue waves
Barbecues, parties and discos
But best of all school holidays.

In autumn the leaves will fall from the trees,
And the wind will blow hard and strong,
Crunch goes the sound of feet on the leaves,
Winter is a time for central heating,
Warm fires and hot cups of tea!

Kirsty Humphrey (11)
Ash Green School

SPORT

Sport is fast, furious, slow and deliberate.
Anyone can play a sport of some sort.

Lee Bennett (13)
Ash Green School

RUNAWAY

The young girl on the stairs,
Listening to the shouting below,
All her life she has listened to the screams,
And now it's time to go.

She clutches her bag,
And heads for the door,
She can't bear her mother's crying,
And her father's shouting anymore.

She quietly opens the door,
While her heart beats fast.
It's time for a wonderful future,
And to leave the devastating past.

She doesn't want to hurt them,
For she's not the hurting kind,
But she has to leave
Yes, she knows that it's time.

She starts to run
And reaches the end of her lane.
Her head is thumping,
And her heart is in pain.

She looks on to her new life.
The new graceful place.
Yet she turns back
And waves goodbye to the nightmare place.

Natalie Taylor (14)
Ash Green School

THE GREAT DAY

Subtle, fresh and relaxing
open fields, no one in sight
just me and my horses
a scattering of white birds in flight
huge white clouds with the
sun beaming through
just me and my horses walking
all day long.
The sun is out and shining
shining on us
Subtle, fresh and relaxing
just me and my horses
with no one in sight.

Paul Clarke (15)
Ash Green School

SKEGNESS

Skegness is so bracing,
It makes me feel so bright.
The wind is so fearfully racing,
It sometimes gives me a fright!
The beach is so soft and yellow,
The sea is so calm and mellow.
I like to breathe so freely,
And to lie and admire the scenery!
Eventually it's time to pack my things,
And carry myself back home!
I've enjoyed my day in Skegness,
But now it's time for my rest!

Emma Hope (14)
Ash Green School

LIFE INSIDE A POSTCARD

'It's quicker by rail',
Is the slogan right now,
But where did it come from?
Why? When? How?

People walking to and fro,
You can't imagine what they know,
About this place,
Which looks so friendly and full of grace,

Their colourful clothes that they wear,
Matches the colour of the hats on their hair,
So now we leave this lively place,
That's so friendly and full of grace.

Nicola Claire Taylor (14)
Ash Green School

MY TEACHER, MRS BAP

My teacher is Mrs Bap
she is so grumpy she made me run a lap.
I asked if I could move class.
The teacher said no! But you are not the only
one to ask.
My teacher Mrs Bap teaches French,
But I would rather sit bored on a bench.
She told me to give in my homework but it
was due in 10 days from now,
I would much prefer Miss How.
One year later she is not that bad,
but now I have Mrs Glad,
She is not like her name,
She is quite sad.

Fiona Marley (11)
Ash Green School

Father And Son

Ever heard of crime my son
robberies and raids?
Ever heard of drugs my son
Syringes, drugs and blades?

'Listen son' take my advice
don't be nasty
try to be nice.
Oh do behave
and do be polite
stay out of trouble
try to do right.
Live your life to its full potential,
don't do anything too regretful.
Don't be forced into anything
you don't want to do,
after all it's your life to live or to lose.

Life's like a football final my son,
you only have one chance.
But if you strive and persist my son
and take that only chance
You'll gain the respect
of others my son.
Your future it will enhance.

There will come a time
when I am gone.
But hopefully you'll pass this advice on.
to future generations of children
like you
After all it's their life
to live or to lose.

Christopher Howard (12)
Ash Green School

THE MASK OF DEATH

The lights are shining on him,
shining on his mask.
Death comes to everyone but not
everyone serves their task.

The gold upon his manly chest
glistens in the light.
The stiffness of his body reflects
every sight.

The atmosphere still, empty dry
air.
He's is all on his own with
no one to care.

Gemma Hurley (14)
Ash Green School

KING OF STONE

Black, white, grey with shadows,
very rough and sharp just like a
barrow.
The sound of the wind
howling like a dog.
Staring´eyes forever and ever,
Cold, dark, mysterious face
reminds me of a king
from a time long ago.

William Burbury (14)
Ash Green School

I Think I Feel Happy!

I started off sad,
Then suddenly out of the blue,
my mouth started to twitch,
Then my eyes started to get really wide,
And my cheeks started to
get higher and higher
and really chubby.
Then my mouth wanted to curve,
So I let it, but only a little bit.
Then just when I think that's it,
I start to feel something,
Then I remember,
I feel joyful.
Then I feel something else,
but I know what this one is,
It is weirdness,
I feel weird.
Then at last I know what I feel.
I feel very, very
Happy!

Rachel Price (11)
Ash Green School

The Musketeers

Black and white,
orange and yellow,
the tough surface holds
a picture of the olden days
reminding me of the Three Musketeers.

Michael Wong (14)
Ash Green School

The Beggar Child

The beggar child so sad and frightened
staring down at her bare feet,
She heaves a sigh which sends the leaves swirling
round her feet,
She is all alone!

She is a beggar-child who sleeps on rags and
doorsteps.
She can run like a deer,
Can climb like a monkey!
She is a pretty girl, just poor!
Her story is a sad one, she is an orphan.

Faye Huxford (11)
Ash Green School

My Cat

My cat can be a pain,
Sometimes I think he's insane.
He looks at me with those big sad eyes,
He likes to eat spiders, moths and flies.
He has little white paws,
And really sharp claws.
His teeth are sharp and gleaming white,
He likes to watch the birds in flight.
He runs round like a maniac,
He's scared to death of the vac.
He's black and white,
He has good sight.
As soon as we met,
I knew he'd be my pet.
He always gets the blame,
And Cas is his name.

Sally Bedford (13)
Ash Green School

SUMMER, WINTER!

Summer has come and winter has gone,
In goes the Christmas trees and out goes the swan,
Summer is bright, hot and cheerful,
Winter is cold, horrible and dullful.

Winter is cold with footprints in the snow,
Summer is warm, with everyone enjoying it,
Robins come out in the winter,
Magpies join us in the summer.

Summer you wear shorts and T-shirt,
Winter you wear trousers and jumpers,
Summer is no coat at no time,
Winter is coat at all times.

Winter looks dull with no leaves on the trees,
Summer is brill with trees full of leaves,
Winter is cold with the frozen grass,
Summer is warm with grass growing quickly

Natasha Bishop (11)
Ash Green School

LUCY

Lucy is white
Lucy has a long pink tail
Lucy is small
Lucy is long
Lucy is a pet
Lucy is a rodent
Lucy is my best friend
Do you know what Lucy is?
Lucy is a
Rat.

Victoria Worwood (11)
Ash Green School

Dolphins

There once was an old man
Who went fishing one day.
He saw a *dolphin* swimming away.

Splish, splash away he goes
He splashes water with his nose.

The old man came from Japan
He chased the *dolphin*
As fast as he can.

He threw out the net
And put on a bet.
To get the *dolphin* as a pet.

The old man gave it such a scare.
I think that he better
Beware!

Sarah Cattermore (11)
Ash Green School

Weekdays

Sunday I go to the swimming pool.
Monday I go back to school.
Tuesday I find 50p.
Wednesday I do PE
On Thursday it was really cool
because I go to see
Arsenal against Liverpool.
On Friday I fly off to Spain.
On Saturday I come back again.

Christopher Knight (12)
Ash Green School

Weather

When I look out of the window, I see,
The thick white snow, like the icing on a cake.
Now I look back on the summer and me,
And all the things we did by the lake.

When I look out of the window, I see,
All of the leaves dropping off the trees.
The crushing of the leaves being stood on,
makes me shiver.

When I look out of the window, I see,
The birds in the trees are singing.
The buzzing of the bees,
And the swaying of the trees.

When I look out of the window, I see,
The sun shining brightly in my eyes.
The grass swaying in the light summer breeze,
It makes summer the nicest I've seen.

Sophie Boulstridge (11)
Ash Green School

Anorexic

I was anorexic once
I could not eat
I tried and tried but
in the end
my friends were
there for me.
They're the ones who
saved me
before it was too late.

Claire Morris (14)
Ash Green School

Excitement Eve

Dozing on a Christmas eve,
Excitement fills my overwhelmed mind
Christmas day just an hour from now,
Advancing into a hidden trance.

My stocking is hung on the fireplace,
Waiting for Santa to fill it with his joy,
The Christmas tree is submerged with decorative ornaments,
Intact baubles hang elegantly, shining in the midnight moonlight.

The clock strikes midnight,
Filling the air with laughter and light,
Every place is festive and ecstatic,
As the children pull open sleek wrapping paper
off their presents.

Candles crackle as the snow shines gracefully,
And the wind blows against the now, white treetops.
This Christmas is by far the best!

John Wragg (11)
Ash Green School

Black, Brown And White!

I wonder why people can be black, brown and white,
Because of this there are fights,
Racism happens to a lot of us,
It happens to people even from their brothers,
Life isn't fair, because lots of people do not care.
What's the difference if we are black, brown or white.
People bully others for unusual things,
Don't they know what a friend really means.

Jenna Jones (13)
Ash Green School

FOOTBALL IS LIKE A DREAM

Football is like a dream
Scoring goals make you gleam.
    You run and pass,
    Shoot and save,
    Shoot and score!
Peep goes the referee's whistle.
    Free kick
    Foul
    Throw in
    Corner
    Offside
    Penalty!
Everyone's on the edge of the seat.
Up goes the red card
And the 'sky-blues' cheer.
Then it's handshakes and autographs,
enjoying the score and knowing that
Coventry are simply the best.

Graeme Taylor (13)
Ash Green School

THE FAMILY

The colours are bright
and the clothes are old
like going to church
or enjoying a walk.

Blues and oranges
Greens and reds
Shadows not many
Lights on their heads.

Rachel Ford
Ash Green School

Love

Love is a very big word
And is not to be said unless meant,
But people say it all the time,
As though it's a daily event.
When people tell you they love you,
They sometimes say it for fun
And then they leave you and run,
Never to return and see what they've done.

Love is a very strong word.
It is meant to last for eternity.
Not everyone sees it that way.
They say that sometimes they're led astray,
But the feeling inside never goes away.

Love is a word that is often heard
By many thoughtful people.
But then again it is also said
By the untruthful.

Star Powell (13)
Ash Green School

An Awesome Sight!

One dark night when the stars were bright
I came across an awesome sight.
Its tail swishing and its wings flapping
I thought to myself what on earth is happening.
There it stood as tall as could be
A great big dragon for all to see.

Jodie Twigger (12)
Ash Green School

WHAT IS LOVE?

To Adam,

Love is as graceful as a dove
What a word 'Love'
As I write this rhyme
I'll commit a crime
do everything for you
Now I say
that I shall pray
that one day God above
will grant us love
so we can be as graceful as a dove.

Natalie Hancocks (12)
Ash Green School

AUTUMN LEAVES

I was walking down the street
Looking at my feet when a
Brown leaf dropped just in
Front of me.
So I looked up, saw an old tree
And I felt really happy.
Rattle rattle went the sound
Of
The petals on the blossom
Tree.
Then lots of leaves fell in
Front of me.

Adam Fripp (11)
Ash Green School

Stressed

My sister turned off my computer
just when it was getting good
I was so angry
I went downstairs
and the TV had broken
I was so angry
I went into the kitchen
to get some crisps
My dad dived and got them
before I could.
I went to get a biscuit
but the dog ate if first
I was so angry
I went to the shop
but the shop was closed
so I went to bed *stressed!*

Gary Taylor (11)
Ash Green School

Cold

As my bones chatter
And my fingers start to freeze
With icicles hanging from my nose
And a shiver down my spine
My toes feel like cardboard
My hands are blue
My nose is red and runny
My ears tingle
My teeth shake in all directions
My body feels like a rock stuck in the ice
And my mind is icing over.

Shelly Baynham (12)
Ash Green School

HAPPINESS

When I feel happy
I'm full of joy inside
I feel like I've been
Asleep for ages and
I've got loads of
Happiness and joy
From dreaming.
I go outside and
See people who are
Sad, I smile at them
And say hello.
They walk off
With a smile
On their face and
It makes me smile
Even more.
I see people sad,
I see people angry,
But I am always
Happy!
I look in the mirror
And see me smiling.
I am smiling all day,
I am smiling all night.
I am smiling when I go to bed,
I am smiling when I wake up.
I am happy all day,
I am happy all night.

I am happy all the time.

Vikki Charlton (11)
Ash Green School

WHAT I THINK OF MY GRAN

As I sit wondering what my gran is doing,
lots of ideas go passing through my head.
She may be knitting, sitting, sewing
or laying in her bed.
Her skin has gone all wrinkly and she's
full of aches and pains.
She's got knobbly knees and bunions,
and she can never remember names.
She's very kind and gentle.
She's got yellow hair like hay.
Her dresses are all flowery
and she brightens up my day.

Kimberley Stokes (12)
Ash Green School

LONDON

Floating away along the tides,
St Paul's above the city rides,
The blue and whites that blend
together,
Below the cathedral which will stand
forever.
And the dull, silent boats, which
pass it by,
Are no longer accompanied with
birds in the sky,
And as this day draws near
to dusk,
Some people come out to busk.

Ruth Forster (14)
Ash Green School

Luke Versus Vader

'Stay calm,' Luke thinks,
As light sabres clash in the
Carbon freezing chamber.

Luke shatters Vader's shield
Then the battle turns to the dark side.
Luke falls towards the chamber
Just escaping Vader's grasp.

The battle rages on into the cargo area.
Vader uses the Force
To knock Luke off course.

Then they reach the edge of the city.
On the bridge, Luke engages with Vader.
The dark one severs Luke's hand and stops,
realising, 'I'm Luke's father.'

Andrew Freeman (14)
Ash Green School

Flying Horse

*R*unning away through the magic forest,
A magical horse glowing in the crescent,
A mystical devotion to the other parts,
*Y*es you must respect the arts,
*O*f this mysterious creature type,
*H*e wanders around with not a creature in sight,
*T*he moonlight shines down,
*W*ith glistening blue all around,
*A*nd settles for the night,
*I*n the magic moonlight.

Becky Beddows (14)
Ash Green School

WAITING FOR A LETTER

I was in the kitchen all alone
Sitting with my cup of tea.
I was shaking like mad.
I kept on looking at the
Clock and then the letterbox.
The sweat was falling off me.

But then I heard footsteps
Coming up the garden,
Was this it?
A letter came through the letterbox
I picked it up and read it
It said 'Yes!'
I ran around the house screaming!

Jenny Milligen (11)
Ash Green School

SCARED

Hiding in your closet,
Noises everywhere,
Gritting teeth, nail biting,
Hiding everywhere,
Scared in dark, really really a lark,
It's got to be scary, in the dark,
Creaking windows,
Creaking stairs,
My poem's about scare.

Mark Harrison (12)
Ash Green School

SANDY
(Dedicated to Sandy Allchin)

Sandy was my dog,
He was a golden retriever
He was so lovely,
With his big brown eyes,
And golden fur.
He never did that much,
Just slept and ate.
He loved to be fussed.
I loved my dog to bits.
Then he became ill,
He had a bad heart.
We went on holiday,
I said goodbye to him,
I never thought it would be the last.

Lorraine Allchin (11)
Ash Green School

FOOTBALL

F or two teams it's Judgement Day.
O ld Trafford is the place they play.
O ld supporters and young people too.
T housands of people all around you.
B e with one team or be with the other
A nxious supporters even your mother.
L ooking at all the fans,
L ouie the keeper lets the ball
slip through his hands.

Andrew Hyland (11)
Ash Green School

My Birthday

B ouncing happily out of bed

I nto the bathroom, splashing my
lazy eyes to wake myself up.

R unning down the thirteen stairs

T earing open the presents

H appily running into the kitchen,
hugging mum, thanking her for
all my presents.

D ay goes on and the clock
strikes three, everyone comes at
half-past three.

A round the kitchen mum runs
trying to get the house ready.
The clock says 3.30pm, mum has finished.

Y asmin arrives, behind her is Lizzy
and everyone else is running down the road

This is going to be a good party.

Leanne Kennedy (11)
Ash Green School

Jumping With Joy

I get up in the morning,
Jumping with delight,

I get myself dressed,
Rushing with happiness.

Cleaning my teeth with
glee, that's what makes
me happy.

Racing to get to school,

English is my first lesson
I'm really really excited.

Art is the best 'cause
I like it best, you discover.

Holly Edgington (11)
Ash Green School

World War III

World War III is a bad place to be,
People dying next to me.
I hope and pray the end will come!

Tanks to the left, tanks to the right,
Bombs all around they give me a fright.
I hope and pray the end will come!

I hope and hope I stay alive
to see my darling wife arrive.
I hope and pray the end will come!

The enemy bring out the cheery bomb,
Suddenly they all seem gone.
I hope and pray the end will come!

They went to the place below,
our work is done and we can go.
I hope and pray the end has come!

Hip, hip hooray, hip, hip hooray!

Neil Sands (12)
Ash Green School

Place Of The Unknown

This faraway place which is now unknown,
Stands upon a hill, quiet and alone,
Was it a castle for a king and queen?
Was it built just to be seen?
Its cold, dull stone which was once a defence,
Now gives off an eerie sense,
With the sky blue and the grass green,
It's hard to imagine all that it has seen.
But for now it will remain alone,
Standing upon a hill,
quiet, dull and unknown.

Sarah Klaassen (14)
Ash Green School

Sport

S occer is the best sport ever!
P assing is the key to success
O ver 45 minutes of pure skill to be
played each half.
R eferee blows the end of the game
T eams leave the field to go and celebrate
or change!

Chris Nuznyi (14)
Ash Green School

WHICH WAY SHOULD THEY GO?

A strange place he does not know,
Which way should he turn? Where should he go?
A man on foot guides the way,
The horse behind pulls the cart all day.
The sun is hot and the air is dry,
The man raises his arms as if to ask why.
The streets are crowded with unknown faces,
Signposts pointing to unfamiliar places,
Which way should they turn? Where should they go?
In this place they do not know.

Andrea Barber (14)
Ash Green School

BLUE

Blue is the colour of the sky
Blue is the colour of the sea
And blue is the colour I write in
And when you are ill you feel blue
And blue is the colour of my science
and English books.
And as you can guess, my favourite colour is
Blue!

Stuart Nash (11)
Ash Green School

The Seasons

Leafless trees
  Animals are gone
    Snow and rain
      That's winter.

Flowers that grow
  A longer day
    New hay
      That's summer.

Dayless chill
  Waking animals
    That's spring.

Golden leaves
  Skies less bright
    Shorter days
      That's autumn.

Francesca Bentley (11)
Barr's Hill Comprehensive School

The Dolphin

The mystical and magical dolphin
Leaps out of the clear blue water
With its wonderful blends of blues and greys
Hearing their soft echoes.
Higher and higher they leap
More and more splashes made
What wonderful animals
Leaving their gentle touch behind for everyone
Singing their soft music
Whooshing their way through the water
As they go beeping along.

Kreeshna Rana (12)
Barr's Hill Comprehensive School

Hallowe'en Night

Hallowe'en night
It gives me a fright
I'm scared in the night.
I can hear eerie sounds
behind my bedroom door.
so I hide under my covers
waiting for fate to creep upon me.
I wait and I wait
Just then I hear my door open bit by bit
I screamed
But it was only my mum
What a relief it was for me
It wasn't a ghost or a witch you see.

Stacey Yates (11)
Barr's Hill Comprehensive School

Sisters

Sisters
Why are sisters such a pain
Sometimes I wonder if they are insane
We always fight every day,
My mum tells us to stop and play.

She always nags and takes my stuff
So I hit her hard, my dad tells me I'm
far too rough
'Now behave girls' my mum nags, 'else you
will go to your room.'
I wish my sister would learn, after all she'll be
eleven soon.

Oh sisters, sisters, sisters, they are such a pain.
I love her dearly, that's the truth really.

Selina Marks (12)
Barr's Hill Comprehensive School

My Football Poem

Football, football,
is my game.

I would love to play
for Coventry.

I would love to score
a hat trick

Against Juventus
in the finals of the
Champions League.

Lloyd Wright (12)
Caludon Castle School

The Cat

There is a soft gentle sound going tip, tip, pat,
Going down the windy stairs is a small, tiny cat.
He rubs his soft head on a nearby chair,
He makes high purrs, that can be heard anywhere.
He jumps on the chair and knocks off a book
His face almost smiling with a mischievous look,
Climbing on the table, so he can get a sight,
Of a chunk of meat, waiting for his bite,
So off the table he did jump,
In his mouth was a chicken lump,
His round, small, green eyes gazed up at the moon,
And he was asleep very soon.

Lorraine Park (12)
Caludon Castle School

The Gift

I'll lend you for a little while a child
of mine, God said,
For you to love while he lives, and mourn
for when he's dead.
It may be six or seven years or forty-two
or three,
But will you, till I call him back, look
after him for me?
He'll bring his charms to gladden you
And should his stay be brief,
You'll always have his memories as
comfort in your grief.

Laura Howell (13)
Caludon Castle School

The Tackle

As the crowd shouts with all
their might
With blue hats and scarves
too
The players fight for every
ball
A player slides along the
turf
And lashes out on the player
with the ball
The injured player stretchered
off
The ref shows the red card
to the guilty player.

Richard Podmore (12)
Caludon Castle School

Steel Band

I like a steel band and
it makes a nice sound.
I play on Tuesdays and Wednesdays
and there's nothing I'd rather do.
You get to go to the concerts
and raise money and wear
cool track suits.

That's why I like a:
Steel Band!

Kirsty Jeremiah (12)
Caludon Castle School

LEFT BEHIND

He was so bright, so full of fun.
He was always right, never outdone.
I don't know why he did it,
He couldn't cope I suppose.
I always thought he was perfect,
Now I will never know.

We used to sit under the apple tree,
at the end of the street
We would chat about our day,
away from the heat.
I would lie and say my day was great,
But I never knew he would come to this fate.

Now it's too late to apologise,
To take back my lies.
I can't believe he is gone,
It has already seemed so long.
How can I put my feelings into words
When the truth is too hard for me to learn?

Every day seems like a year gone by.
Every night I can't help but cry.
I will never forget you.
You left me behind.

Jessica Ward (12)
Caludon Castle School

My Little Brother

My little brother
Is a boy like no other,
He makes me really mad
because he's very, very bad.

My little brother
Is football crazy,
But sometimes he's lazy,
and he won't do his homework at night.

My little brother
Is really a boy like no other,
He makes me despair
When he's doing his hair,
and can't get in the bathroom at all.

But he's my little brother
and it's just *not fair!*

Emma Whiteley (13)
Caludon Castle School

If I Win The Lottery

Money, money everywhere
Money, money in the air
Everything you ever wanted
Chocolate, sweets and limousines
Money, money everywhere
Money, money in the air.

Claire Godfrey (12)
Caludon Castle School

CANNONBALL CAT

My next-door neighbour's cat
Went chasing after a rat
But the rat was too quick
For the Cannonball Cat.

The Cannonball Cat sat down
Licking its paw
And then the rat
Came running through the door.

The cat jumped up
Taking aim
Pounce
But the rat was too quick
For the Cannonball Cat.

By then the cat was as angry as fire
Hurling at anything
Which came into his eye.

The rat ran off
And so did the cat
Chasing him everywhere
And losing his fat.

When the time came
The cat caught up with the rat
Licking his paws
And putting on fat
Eating his tasty treat.

Hannah Simmons (12)
Caludon Castle School

DREAMS

Every time I go to bed,
I cannot keep thoughts out of my head.
I dream a lot
I cannot stop
Some dreams are nice,
Some are not.

I dream of a world that is so great,
It's full of love but rid of hate.
In my world there would be no
poor people of poverty.
There would be no diseases that
could harm anybody.

I would be rich and famous too,
I would be worth a million of you.
I could have what I wanted,
I could do what I like,
I would buy all my friends a motorbike.

Jamie Agnew (12)
Caludon Castle School

IF ONLY I COULD

I wish to be rich and to have houses and cars.
I would wish for more and more wishes.

My second wish is to give the teachers
a million pounds each not to come to school.

My third wish is to go and travel around the world.
I would go and see Mickey and Minnie in Disneyland.
Go and see Santa at the north pole
And go all round the world.

Sinead Taylor (12)
Caludon Castle School

My Heaven

My imaginary Heaven is way above
The house is white, white as a dove,

The biggest room of them all
Has a throne that's 10ft tall!
Carefully placed is my throne
With my name chipped in, 'Simone'
No one believes me, when I tell them this,
It is all true, I promise you, it's not just a wish!

The kitchen is full of tasty treats,
Cakes, chocolate, jelly and sweets.
The living room is best of all,
Even though it is quite small.
I have 100 TVs in this room
And out of CD players music booms.

My bedroom has a four-poster bed,
The door is made of steel and lead
To keep away an unwelcome sister
Who takes your things and likes to pester.
On my wall there hangs a frame
Of my Dad who's quite insane!

Now what's left to say? Ah yes the Hall,
Dull and brown are the walls,
We haven't had time to decorate.
But don't worry yourselves, it's not too late
I'm not coming up here till later on,
When I'm old, dead and gone!

Simone Parker (13)
Caludon Castle School

The Unicorn

Silver grey in the moonlight,
His horn shining out like a silver sun,
Cantering softly.

Weaving in and out of the glistening trees,
Wistfully, gracefully, energetically.

Pausing only to spread his wings -
Like a blanket of stars.

Jump on! I must jump on!
Soaring on a unicorn, in the moonlight.
The world below us, sleeping, sleeping.

He lands without a thud
Canters then halts.

Jump down, I don't want to, but I must!
He canters, then gallops,
Spreading his blanket of stars
Soaring high above the city.

He'll come back to me,
I know,
My unicorn!

Leanne Haines (13)
Caludon Castle School

The Mouse

There was a little mouse
who lived in Roger's house.
His house was very small
it had a garden wall.

Next door's house had a mate
who used to walk through the
garden gate, to chase the mouse
who lived in Roger's house.

Stephanie Downs (12)
Caludon Castle School

SPRING

In the spring all things seem bright,
They are so full of light,
At night they lie down and rest,
Then wake up to a new day.

All the flowers relax in the warm sun,
They sway side to side in the cool breeze,
It's as if they are laughing when they sway,
Looking as happy as can be.

The little children, all running in the fields,
Playing their games all full of joy,
Some of the children picking daisies,
Making little necklaces for their teachers.

The little baby lambs jumping above,
Leaping from field to field as happy as can be,
Chewing the grass as they bounce,
Playing Tig with their little friends.

At the end of the day everyone is tired,
They all have a relaxing bath,
Wash their hair to keep it nice and wavy,
Then they lie down and think about the happy
things they did.

Katie Wilson (12)
Caludon Castle School

WASHING MACHINE

Wishy, washy, washing machine
Goes round and round,
Making your clothes clean,
So no dirt's to be found.

Open the drawer,
Pour the soap powder in,
Like snowflakes they fall,
Making no din.

It opens its mouth,
And gobbles the lot,
As fast as a lion,
It'll eat all you've got.

Wobbly, a jelly,
It to's and fro's,
Swishing and squashing,
Mashing the clothes.

Gizmos and gadgets,
Buttons galore,
An ape's stomach rumbling
Now it wants more!

First on a rinse,
Now on fast spin,
Pull out the clean clothes,
Put more dirty ones in!

Victoria Bailey (12)
Caludon Castle School

CHEATING CAT

There comes to mind a cat named Buster,
A cheating cat indeed.
He knows tricks and cheats for any game,
All hidden up his sleeve.

From snakes and ladders to bingo and poker,
He knows cheats for every single one.
With a glint of his eye and a flick of his hand,
The game will be over and he's gone.

Nobody knows how Buster does it,
But everybody knows that he plays tricks.
Police have been called to watch over him,
They don't see anything and Buster's gone in a tick.

Buster's a millionaire now from this horrible crime,
And lives in a big white house.
With a beautiful wife and kittens of his own,
With the youngest kitten named Mouse.

Buster always wear a clean black tuxedo,
And his kittens follow in his steps.
They now gamble like their father Buster,
Winning all the games and bets.

There comes to mind a cat named Buster,
A cheating cat indeed.
He knows tricks and cheats for any game,
All hidden up his sleeve.

Seecum Cheung (13)
Caludon Castle School

AUTUMN DELIGHT

As the leaves come falling down
On the fields, on the ground.
The autumn sun shone so bright.
It filled my heart with joy and delight.

Autumn, autumn what's it about?
When all the animals stop coming out.

Leaves on the ground
All crispy and brown.
You get your gloves and your scarf.
You wrap up tight
To beat the cold and crispy night.

Autumn, autumn, what's it about?
When all the animals stop coming out.

Sitting watching the fire at night.
Burning o' so bright.
O' what a wonderful sight.
It fills my heart with joy and delight.

Kaeran Stevens (13)
Caludon Castle School

THE SUMMER

Watch the sun coming out,
Bright red filling the sky,
See the birds fly away in groups,
Whistling as they go by.

The sun is now sweltering,
The sweat is pouring out,
People are begging for drink,
Everyone is dizzy.

Watch the owls hoot at night,
See the branches swing.
Watch the moon shine brightly,
See all the stars come out.

Sarbdeep Sidhu (12)
Caludon Castle School

If I Won The Lottery

If I won the lottery,
Oh how happy I would be,
I would treat my family without a care,
For all the money I would share.
For my dad,
A new car,
He would think,
I'm a star.
For my brother,
A season ticket for his favourite team.
For my mother,
The brand new house of her dreams.
And for myself,
A motorbike,
That shines and gleams,
And every week I would clean,
To make it sparkle,
Spick and span,
Oh dear I forgot about my Nan.
I don't know what I would get for her,
Maybe a coat that's made of fur,
All my friends I would not forget,
But I've not won the money yet.

Steve Hambleton (12)
Caludon Castle School

Me And My Family

Me and my family just running along
When the clock goes ding dong ding dong.
Me and my family just playing about
There's mum's vase
Quick, watch out!

Me and my sister's in hospital now
Quick it's Sky TV turn over, wow!
Bart Simpson for my sisters
Hang Time for me with Chris, Mary-Beth
and soon, there's Susie.

Us out of hospital, no family in there now,
Until I kill my sisters, that's it.

Arragh! Help!

Laura-Jayne Butcher (12)
Caludon Castle School

Heaven

Like a swift bird in the sky,
Sound of a sudden cry,
I look around, feeling lost and alone,
But up, up, up,
In the great white somewhere,
I think there is a heaven up there.
Above clouds as soft as cotton wool,
Heaven is like a spinning ball,
Voices like a choir.
Dancing like a fire,
Ribbons whirling, twirling in the air,
Coming going, like a fading flare.

Vijay Shah (12)
Caludon Castle School

Sisters

Sisters are things that get on your nerves,
Sisters are things that we don't deserve,
They embarrass you in front of your friends,
And nag at you until the day ends.

They always want to give you a kiss,
You dodge out the way and hope they miss,
They rely on you for everything,
And always wear a fake gold ring.

They always want to play with you,
And you really love them through and through,
Although they can be such a pain,
They keep you company when it rains.

They bother you when it's hot,
Because they love you such a lot,
They nag and cry, they scream and shout,
But hey! That's what sisters are all about.

Vicki Morton (13)
Caludon Castle School

The Sun

The sun is as bright as a jewel in the night,
Like a cold spotlight jumping out from
a fluffy black cloud.
It's as round as a football, as fierce as a lion's roar,
Stronger than a female boar.
It's as gold as a new pound coin like a shimmering
lightning bolt coming down in a line,
but if that sun had never become then we would
never be around to see.

Georgina Davies (12)
Caludon Castle School

PUPPY DOG TALES

I have the cutest puppy dog
A darling you'll agree,
Isn't he a lucky thing
To look like little me.

My plumpish doggy doesn't bark -
Please do not get me wrong
How can he use his voice if he
Is eating all day long

Wee Rover is my super-pet
I think he's very bright
As bright as our house when there's
A power cut at night.

A funny looking dog is this
His head is strangely hairy,
And makes a first-class nesting spot
For Sam our pet canary.

A kindly pooch is my pet, Peeps
Known to our postman Fred
She doesn't tear his suit to bits,
But bites his leg instead.

My doggy, Eddy, always takes
A quite short-sighted view.
He once mistook a bar of soap
For toffee - I did too.

Ashley Croft (12)
Caludon Castle School

MONEY!

Money, money, win the lottery.
Money, money, win it twice a week.
Money, money, silver, bronze and gold.
Money, money doesn't grow on trees.
If I had a chance I would bet on a horse
Money, money, wonderful money.
I'd spend it here and there.
Money, money, money
Cars, mansions and a private jet.
Money, money, holidays in Barbados.
Money, money, why save it?
Money, money, spend it while I can.
Money, money, money!

John Hornibrook (12)
Caludon Castle School

FOOTBALL

The crowd cheer as the players trudge out,
Shiny new kit lovely and clean,
'*Peeeep*' as the crowd shout,
The whistle goes for another
ninety muscle-bounding,
ball-skidding mean minutes.
Battered and bruised and all
covered in mud,
they get cheered once again
for the final whistle has gone!

Antony Spelman (12)
Caludon Castle School

UFOs And Space

I am into UFOs
So my poem is about,
Well I think you know.

As I walked down the street,
I looked at the stars,
But couldn't breathe, couldn't speak,
'Cause in the sky, probably from Mars
Was a light, so magnificently bright,
Dancing through the night,
It must have been travelling at the
speed of light.

Then I froze, just stood there
Gazing at the dark sky,
The millennium falcon came to visit,
I must have nearly died,
'Cause Luke, Han, Chewie and Leia were in it.

My mission was to destroy an alien race,
So I jumped at light-speed into outer space,
I didn't want my friends to know,
As I woke, lying in the freezing snow,
But I didn't know I was on another planet,
Until I met an alien called Irranigranite.
I woke again, from my dream,
And on my finger was a ring that gleamed,
It said my mission was to destroy an alien race,
But, no one can hear you scream in *outer space . . . !*

Ian Yale (12)
Caludon Castle School

THE NEW BOY

There was a new boy,
A new boy in town
His hair very white,
Skin very brown,
With a limp like a wounded soldier,
Cat-like eyes which made him look much older
His first day at school;
He tried to settle in
The other children took critical glances at him
They decided to speak to him,
To see what his accent was like
Theirs was very posh, precise, efficient
and always right.
He replied back to them,
In an effort to make a friend
His accent was common, stumbling
and out of a different blend
Presently it got too much,
They decided to take the mickey
With names such as 'Hop Along Cas,' and
'Hill Billy Ricky.'
As bullying always does,
It built and built and built
The names became prejudiced and racist
They left him on edge, on a tilt
Eventually he'd had enough
Of the bullying he'd received
He stood at the top of his block of flats,
He breathed the last breath he would breathe,
He jumped,
He landed,
He never woke up,
Just how he planned it.

Sarah Harriott (12)
Caludon Castle School

THE FROG SPELL

Water lilies and red dye
Frogs' legs and fungi
Lizards' tongues
And newts' tails
Shells of snails
And old dogs' tails
Throw them in and let them boil
Then wrap them up in hot tin foil
When they're done, take them out
Turn around and give a shout
Stuff the mixture in a hog
Then feed it to the person who will
then become a frog.

Jamie Bell (12)
Caludon Castle School

RICHARD'S 'W'S

Window, wind, wig, wire,
Richard's 'W's do inspire!
They are weird, wacky, wild and wonderful,
Take one look and you will be cheerful.

Instead of 'W's they look like 'U's,
Sometimes they leave you very confused!
Richard's 'W's have a life of their own,
Starting from little they have grown.

Like himself they are different,
Richard's 'W's come from Kent,
Window, wind, wig, wire,
Richard's 'W's do inspire.

Katie Shenton (12)
Caludon Castle School

Bullying

Every day I dread going to school to avoid having my blood on the floor in a pool.

'Please!' I say as I beg to stay at home but it makes no difference.

To make the matter worse my mum drives me to school, I insist to walk but that's no good.

Surprisingly, a short journey seems to be turning long seeming like an hour.

We arrive, I get out of the car and start walking but just coming up to the gates I see the bully.

Maybe I can get through the back school gates I think to myself so I turn back and start walking quickly to my destination.

After five paces I hear the warning bell go.

To keep my hundred percent record of not being late I turn and try to run through the front gates.

Uh oh! I've been caught, the pain now begins and it doesn't stop when the bruises disappear but it's for life.

If you want to avoid this do the right thing tell someone.

Gurvinder Mann (12)
Caludon Castle School

Ferrari Vs Atari

I would love a new Ferrari
It will be better than my old Atari.
I'll be going fast down the lane
Better than a computer game.

Craig Tinto (12)
Caludon Castle School

The Sea

I love the sea,
But deary, deary me, what can I see?
I can see a crisp bag floating towards me.
Gone are the days when it was litter-free.

But I still love to see the sea,
Big waves, little waves all dashing towards me,
Sand in my toes, flies up my nose,
Watching the Punch and Judy shows.

Buckets and spades are for me,
Sandcastles with moats, and lots and lots of boats.
Candyfloss, ice cream and a cup of tea,
It's lovely to be beside the sea!

Tara Bate (12)
Caludon Castle School

Football

This is a poem about football,
People screaming, shouting and yelling,
'Go City go!'
Dublin, Dublin, scores again,
When City wins the game,
the ground is full of joy,
but when they lose,
it's such a pity,
especially when the game
was bitty.
I love to watch Coventry
play even on a rainy day.

Emma Shuttleworth (12)
Caludon Castle School

A Poem About Teletubbies

I wake up every morning,
about seven fifteen.
To watch the famous foursome,
on the television screen.

Teletubbies are my favourite
I watch them every school day,
Po, Laa-Laa, Dipsy and Tinky Winky,
come out to play.

The Teletubbies are very bright,
red, yellow, purple and green.
Their telly bellies and tubby toes,
the cutest characters I've ever seen.

Po is my favourite,
she has a circle on her head.
She's the smallest of the group,
and Po's the one who is bright red.

There is another character,
his name is Noo-Noo,
He's a nice vacuum cleaner,
but he's very naughty too.

Every teletubby has to eat,
and they only eat one thing,
They eat tubby custard
so they can dance and sing!

Paula May (12)
Caludon Castle School

Teachers

Teachers, they are funny creatures.
Nice one day, but not the next,
Make you read a weird text.
Yes, that's right
No, that's wrong
Best behaviour all day long.
Who's that shouting?
What's her name?
For goodness sake, not him again!
Shut up Michael,
Sit down Claire,
Then appears the deadly glare.
Eyes get scrunched,
Mouth goes sour,
Dare not argue with so much power.
No one moves, we dare not speak
If we do detentions all week.
Come on bell, start to ring,
We all know the joy you bring.
The day is over the work is done
Let's go home and have some fun.
Oh brilliant, oh great, I just knew!
I'd have two hours of homework to do!

Michelle Darby (12)
Caludon Castle School

Motorsport Poem

What is red?
A car is red, racing ahead of the rest.

What is black?
A tyre wall is black, ready to comfort
a crash.

What is orange?
The reflectors are orange, all nice and
shining.

What is grey?
The smoke of the tyres is grey, at the
start of the race.

Nicholas Nutt (13)
Caludon Castle School

The Washing Machine

The wild, wishy, washy washing machine,
Sat in the kitchen sparkling clean.
It washes your clothes with foam-like shampoo,
To keep them fresh and clean for you.
It wishes and washes and turns around
It can make such an awful sound.

The washing machine shakes like an earthquake,
Like whisking mix to make a cake.
With a rumble and a tumble it rotates around,
With a splish and a splash that is the sound.

The washing machine is a rickety old car,
Which unfortunately, wouldn't get very far.
The washing machine has a clear glass face,
Its brain swirls round like it's in a race.
With a wish and a wash and a whirr, whirr, whirr,
It can even clean a coat that's made of fur.

At the end of the cycle, the spinning finally stopped
The machine ceases working, all the contents have
now flopped.
Its chore is now completed, the clothes are fresh and clean,
So well it does its daily job I'd give it to the queen.

Chloe Darby (13)
Caludon Castle School

Jimmy 'Fat Boy' Johnson

Jimmy 'Fat Boy' Johnson
Is such a friend to me.
He often throws his weight around,
For everyone to see.

He's built just like an army tank,
Almost reaching twenty stone.
With all the junk food he consumes,
No way is he skin and bone!

But beneath his huge fat belly,
Is a sensitive little soul
Who hates all the name-calling,
And has a heart of gold.

He's generous and very giving
And he's loyal to the end.
He's good at keeping secrets,
What more could you have in a friend?

Adam James (12)
Caludon Castle School

My Football Dream

If I could go to the FA Cup Final
I would like to play for Man United
against Arsenal.
I would play with Ryan Giggs and
all the rest of the players
and win the FA Cup with Man United
and score the winning goal.

David Robinson (12)
Caludon Castle School

THE GRUMPY OLD MAN

The grumpy old man
Who lived in a van
A grumpy old man was he
The grumpy old man
Who lived in a van
Collected bottle tops
And old Coke cans
Soon after dinner
His dream came true.
He married a cat
In a big black hat
Who lived with a mouse
As flat as a mat.
The grumpy old man
Who married a cat
With a big black hat
Who lived with a mouse
As flat as a mat.
The little mouse who
Lived with a cat
Who wears a big black hat
Who married a man who
Lived in a van,
And a very grumpy man
was he.

Nicholas Allibone
Caludon Castle School

Machines

You walk into a factory,
You stop and look around.
You hear a small and tiny squeak,
A low and murmuring sound.

You walk closer to the noise,
You wonder what it is.
There's someone in the staff room
Opening the fridge.

You switch on the kettle,
It whistles along with you.
But you just stand there
Wondering what to do.

You reach for the heater switch,
You turn it on with care.
Soon it will be blowing out lovely
Nice hot air

The factory's waking up now,
The machines seems to chatter.
Everyone's coming to work now,
Natter, natter, natter.

You wonder what the machines
Are making,
You go and have a look.
Machines making machines!
I think I'll stick to books.

Jennie Stanley (12)
Caludon Castle School

Love

Love, doesn't it hurt?
Does anything ever go right?
Why me?
You ask yourself all these questions,
Any answers? No!

The one feeling of all,
The one which will always get you down,
The one which will always feel the worst,
And the one which you'll never ever forget.

It breaks your heart,
You cry,
You feel like you've lost everything,
Everything you've ever had.
You want a big hole in the ground to
open up and just swallow you whole.

All you want is for all the hurt to go away,
But will it? No!
It's that feeling,
The one feeling that makes you want to lock
yourself away and never come back.
And what's that feeling?
It's the feeling of being . . . *dumped!*

Vicky Parker (12)
Caludon Castle School

Washing Machine

Open the door,
What do you see?
Dirty clothes
Waiting for me.

Dirty tops
Sweaty socks
Tatty jamas
I'll wash the lot.

Fill up the soap tray,
Turn the dial to start,
In goes the water
Dirt and clothes will part.

When I've stopped spinning
You can open the door
Take out these clean clothes
I'm ready for some more.

Michelle Bulpitt (12)
Caludon Castle School

My Horse Disney

Horses are lovely,
they are lots of fun,
Running round the field,
playing in the sun.

They run round the field,
they gallop around.
My horse is so beautiful,
and I am very proud.

My horse is so lovely
she is the best
She's so good-tempered
so much better than the rest.

Beth Starnes (12)
Caludon Castle School

THE WASHING MACHINE

The washing machine whirled and rumbled
Its insides turned and the clothes tumbled.
The clothes inside are getting washed.
You could see the water as it slipped and sloshed.
The clothes come out, it settles down
They're as clean as a whistle, they won't
make you frown.

The next load goes in as it opens its mouth
The shirts fly north, the socks swim south.
What's that noise in the bubble and froth
Oh, it's alright, just a button came off.

The machine speeds up, it starts spinning faster.
Some water spills out, what a disaster.
The water is still coming, the cat's bowl is floating.
Everywhere is wet - the carpet is soaking.
We call out the plumber - he puts it right
The end of the wash is now in sight.

The machine goes quiet - the last cycle ceases.
It's over to mum to iron out the creases
The machine has a rest now, till the next time around
What's that in the drum, oh, a clean shiny pound.

Lisa Jones (11)
Caludon Castle School

Tiger Food

Tiger, tiger, burning bright
What are you gonna eat tonight?
A nice kebab may be OK
You might prefer a take-away!

Tiger, tiger, burning bright
What are you gonna eat tonight?
Perhaps some tasty fried giraffe
You could ambush a rhino, in the bath!

Tiger, tiger, burning bright
What are you gonna eat tonight?
You may like to have some nice beef stew
Don't try the lion 'cos it'll eat you!
Tiger, tiger, burning bright,
what you gonna eat tonight?

Craig Worrall (12)
Caludon Castle School

My Pony

She has a long silky black mane.
She has a thick coat that
keeps her warm.
She goes at speed and she's no need
to stop.
She kicks and squeals with anger.
She's my pony *Hannah!*
And she the best!

Eleanor Hobday (12)
Caludon Castle School

A Poem About A Poem

You're asked to write a poem OK
So what about?
You sit and think,
Your mind's spinning
Like a hurricane,
Like water swirling down the sink,
Slowly all your ideas flow away,
down the drain.

Then it suddenly comes to you,
Like a light being switched on.
'Click'
So now you've got an idea.
You've got to decide what to write in it.
So you thought you were getting somewhere,
but no!
You're punched straight back to square one.
No idea, not one, not one single tiny idea.

So what have you learnt all this time . . .
. . . that a poem's hard to write?
Yes! Yes!
That's it, that's what you learnt
That a poem's hard to write.
So, why not write a poem about . . .
a poem!

Nichola Brown (13)
Caludon Castle School

Hockey

Hockey, hockey, hockey
can't get enough of it.
Hockey hockey, hockey, eat sleep
and drink it.
Hockey, hockey, hockey, wind up and
shoot it.
Hockey, hockey, hockey,
can't forget about it

h y
o e
c k
k c
e o
y h

Hockey!

Wesley McCranor (12)
Caludon Castle School

As Time Goes By . . .

As time goes by, people pass my house.
First the milkman, then the paperboy.
Finally a salesman who wants me to buy a door.

As time goes by, the day passes my house.
First the wind, then the rain.
Finally the sun which dries up the water.

As time goes by, vehicles pass my house.
First five cars, then three vans.
Finally a great big lorry.

As time goes by, animals pass my house.
First a cat, then a dog.
Finally a fox, which chases the cat and dog.

Stephen McNulty (12)
Caludon Castle School

THE TROUBLESOME TRACTION ENGINE

Terence the troublesome traction engine
tricks the other traction engines.
They think he is so very mean perhaps
they might start a team.

Terence is a mean, keen tricking machine.
When the engines are clean he is very keen
to take off the sheen.

However the engines try they can't trick
Terence the traction engine. Then one day
they hear him scream. They chug to his rescue
but only to see him clean.

Then the other engines take the mick.
They call 'Now you know what it's like to
take the stick.'

Dale Duncombe (12)
Caludon Castle School

School

School is boring
Yeah especially Maths
I have to wake up early in the morning
Earlier than me dad.

School has too many tests
Yeah with weird names of them
My school's got its own crest
What's a crest?

School takes too long
That makes it more boring
In music you have to sing rubbish songs
Yeah Swan Lake, I fell asleep singing.

School has many teachers
Yeah, too many weird names to remember
In science we see weird little creatures
Ya mean the tiny little things.

School makes you do homework
There's too much of that
In history we learn about warrior Turks
Who are they?

So I guess I'm saying school is boring?
Yeah Maths and all that.

Robert Hewitt (13)
Caludon Castle School

Rebellious Girl

Take a look at your life, what do you see?
An innocent schoolgirl or a trashy Spice Girls wannabe?
If I were to answer that question for you,
I assure you I would pick option two.
I thought we'd be friends forever but you decided to change,
You walk around like you're the best thing going
and I am out of your range.
Your new platinum blonde hair with its myriad of black roots,
Sets of your new image perfectly with those Doc Marten boots.
I just adore your dress sense, is the grunge look in
It suits your bad reputation like a second skin,
You've adopted drinking and smoking as your two new themes,
Don't you realise your life is splitting at the seams?
You've nothing to be proud of, what's the point of your life?
All you ever do is cause trouble and strife.
You used to be popular. You used to have friends,
Why don't you try to make amends?
You turned on us for no apparent reason at all,
Are you really so petty and small?
If you're so popular, where are all your friends?
They're only there when you have money to spend.
You buy them cigarettes and drink,
Have you ever taken the time to stop and think?
However tough things are, true friends will always be there,
Believe it or not we actually care.
I don't know what changed you, your life used to be so clear,
Now you're an enigma partly through fear.
You think you're as special as a freshwater pearl,
But you're nothing but a conceited jumped-up, *rebellious girl!*

Emma Smith (14)
Ernesford Grange

BEING THE MIDDLE ONE

Being the middle one is
awfully hard for me
My dad loves my elder brother,
and my mum loves my younger sister
Nobody loves me.

My gran is the only one
who actually seems to care
She listens to my worries
and helps me through the day,
but she's got her own life too
She can't listen to me chattering, chattering away.

I'm nothing to my family
They don't really care.
I have a life too, I'll do what I want
I'm only twelve but I get treated
too much like an adult.

They need me only
when there's housework to do
My brother can't do it
because he's always too busy
and my sister can't do it
because she's too small.

So therefore you see
I'm totally lonely
My whole family has other things to do

Except for being a family to me!

Jamini Pankhania (11)
Sidney Stringer CTC School

Looking For A Nightingale

As I walk,
around my garden,
I stop to look,
listen and pardon,
the nightingale,
as he goes his way,
his wings stretched out,
to greet the day.

As he swoops,
towards the ground,
he stops and looks,
above his crown,
he spreads his dew,
like falling rain,
their smell and beauty,
gives pleasure and pain.

I have a garden,
full of flowers,
reminding me of,
friendships and hope,
each flower unequalled,
in its own prettiness and grace,
and where I find the rose bush,
I hope I find the nightingale.

Jeanne Anne Tierney (11)
Sidney Stringer CTC School

Cries For Help

It's hard to cry for help, walking down a dark, cold, windy street with evil eyes looking at you. Crowds of people against you, some wicked, some cruel, you don't know what will happen!

While you walk into the crowd, you can see the knives, spanners, and other tools in their hands, behind their backs, in their pockets, hidden in boxes.

After you separate desperately, you can see and hear them behind you, making large thumping noises.
More and more ganging against you shouting *'Down with that mick!'*

The quicker I walk the quicker they follow, I hide in the scrap yard wishing I had a super hero, who could save me.

When they got me, I felt the large thumps and as quick as a flash I was down, I could feel their feet kicking me and hitting me with anything, with all their anger, just because I'm a Catholic.

When they had finished me off, I knew I couldn't walk down those streets again, without crying for help.

Ahmed Mangera (13)
Sidney Stringer CTC School

Poetry

Poetry is poetry.
It may be good.
It may be bad.
It may be happy.
It may be sad.

Some like poetry.
Some detest it.
Some write it beautifully.
By now you must have guessed it.

Babak Knonsorkh (11)
Sidney Stringer CTC School

SCHOOL

When you break up from primary
that can be very sad,
Even though you are very glad
to be going to big school.
Older kids often say it's very cool
to be going to secondary school
then all of a sudden last-minute nerves
come and then you think
what if my friends don't want to go there anymore
and then you try to calm
yourself and say I've made new friends anyway
and then you hear all kinds
of rumours like they tie your shoelaces together
and flush your head down the toilets
and older kids bullying the 1st years and then you
speak to all your friends and they say that
they're scared to just stick with your
friends and they'll stick with you and when you finally get
there you find out that they were just kidding.

Iarnah Dennis (11)
Sidney Stringer CTC School

VILLAGE CRICKET

Beer-bellied bowler
bowls.
Batsman drives ball to
boundary,
Umpire indicates,
Scoreboard clicks.

Beer-bellied bowler
bowls
Batsman drives -
uncertainly,
Bails flick,
Bowler celebrates.

Batsman walks shaking head,
Fielders cheer.

Javed Sheikh (11)
Sidney Stringer CTC School

THINK TWICE

Sometimes I wish I was never born
because of little arguments.
Then I think about other people
who are worse off than me.
I've got food, clothing and shelter
while others have none of this.
I've got a family that loves me
and I shouldn't take advantage of that.
So next time I wish I was never born
I'll think again, twice as hard.

Kamaljit Shankerwalia (13)
Sidney Stringer CTC School

The Unseen World

I saw her once on the street
curled up tight with nothing to eat.
She wrapped the blanket
around her body, so thin and small,
hoping it would keep her warm.
I saw the beauty behind that dirty face,
so cold and fragile with nothing
left to face.
I saw the light in her eyes
when a person passes her by
who would throw a penny or two
for her, it probably smelt like food.
I once sat here, and watched all
the people, who walked by.
Not caring for the girl with tears
in her eyes.
With no food, no home, and
completely alone.
So I stand here feeling helplessly ashamed,
knowing I could have saved her
from this wicked day.
Now I'm left to see her body so cold and pale.
With an innocent expression on her face
leaving me hoping that she is now in
a better place.

Sazna Khatun (13)
Sidney Stringer CTC School

The Love Poem

There's a special place
here in my heart
For the one I have loved
right from the start
One two, I love you
three four, I want more
It's not just what you've done for me
that makes me love you so
It's all the joy of who you are
the friend I've come to know
One two, I love you
three four, I want more
My heart is like a cabbage
divided into two
I give the leaves to others
and I give the heart to you.
One two, I love you
three four, I want more
Over the ocean
across the sea
leave everything
and come to *me!*
One two, I love you
three four, I want more.

Aisha Khalifa (13)
Sidney Stringer CTC School

Feelings On Seasons

Pain is like winter
with cold and hurt all around
where sadness spreads like butter
on toast,
with people putting you down.
    Pain is like winter.

Love is like spring
with new things happening
never knowing what comes next,
but hopefully joy.
    Love is like spring

Happiness is like summer
no more school or work,
playing in the sun,
going to the beach.
    Happiness is like summer

Being afraid is like autumn
when pain and fun collide
with Halloween coming soon
with witches and ghosts,
singing and dancing under a full moon.
    Being afraid is like autumn.

Steven Busby (13)
Sidney Stringer CTC School

The Midnight Nightmare

I suddenly awake from a midnight nightmare, where I am trapped in
my own unconsciousness.
It is the dead of the night and all is asleep, except me.
I lie there alone scared, frightened unable to move, paralysed with fear.
The accounts of the nightmare keep re-running in my mind, over and
over and over again.
As if I was watching a movie for the hundredth time.
All is still and quiet, but in the distance I hear footsteps and a creaky
door opens.
I freeze, paralysed, frightened to death. I lie there unable to move, my
body nerves have frozen.
I feel as if I am under the red-hot boiling sun, with a duvet over me.
I feel as if I'm drowning beneath a sea of sweat, but only to realise
it's my blankets.
My mind in shock, from a sudden dream to total awareness.
My eyes are the only part of my body capable of moving, the rest of
me feels numb and dead.
Like radar scanners they scan the room, looking for something I'm
not too sure is there.
I'm making shadows out of the darkness, watching them coming
towards me.
I hear another sound, I can feel my heart racing so fast like it wants
to escape from my body.
I want this feeling to go away, but it wants to stay.
I lie there all night, hoping someone will come to my rescue, but
no one comes.
I just lie there, all night in the same position, until the sun comes up
and brings light into my room.
I then suddenly feel safe and that nothing can harm me now,
and the light softly and gently, but eventually rocks me to
sleep.

Inderjeet Banwait (16)
Sidney Stringer CTC School

LOVE OR FRIENDSHIP

Ever since I met you
nothing in life has been the same,
but I want to give it up here
and I want to forget this game.
How many nights I sit here, with love on my mind.
I can't forget your smile or the way your eyes linger
I have always wanted to express my love
to show you how I really feel,
but something deep inside stops me
because I do not know your deal.
I always thought you would be mine one day
but when you went, my dreams ran away.
I do not want you back for a weekend,
I don't want you back for a day,
I want you in my life again
and this time I want you to stay.
I do not want you back as my lover
but as my loyal friend
and every time you need my help
I will be willing to lend a hand.
I'll be there for you, through the happy and sad
and through the thick and thin,
I will always be by your side
just as you wanted me to be, as a good friend.

Kamaljit Sidhu (16)
Sidney Stringer CTC School

Spooky Ghosts

Do you see those ghosts? Well I do!
I see them in the dark.
I see them in the light.
I see them in the day.
And I see them in the night . . .
All of a sudden I started to shrink.
All I could see was pink, pink, pink.
I shrank in a corner, then I went
to the door, it was locked. The ghost
came closer and in his hands was
a hot splot of gore, he spat it
in my face, I screamed, nobody came
I was alone, with his beam.
I wished it was a dream, I rubbed
the gore from my face and I rubbed
my eyes, but it would not go away!

Aamena Kola (11)
Sidney Stringer CTC School

Myself

I am a girl who lives in a house, in a house I do,
I work all day, and get my pay and have my rest
and wake up the next day.
I am a girl who lives in a house, in a house I do,
I'm grumpy, I'm kind, I'm bossy, I'm fine, that is all
I do.
I am a girl who lives in a house, in a house I do,
I love my mum, I love my dad, I love my brothers too.
I am a girl who lives in a house, in a house I do,
I play outside and come inside and start my work like you.
I am a girl who lives in a house in a house I do.

Nilam Jussab (11)
Sidney Stringer CTC School

Myself

I am a girl called Nabila Sheikh,
I live in Coventry and go to school
for the day.
My mum thinks my intelligence
is great in school.
I have my parents and my
sisters too,
I have no brothers but that's
nothing new.
I'm helpful, naughty, and bossy
I'm grumpy, clumsy, and also
lazy,
I'm very chubby, but who really
cares,
Me and my food are always a pair.

Nabila Anwer Sheikh (11)
Sidney Stringer CTC School

Nightmares

Nightmares, nightmares, nightmares.
I cannot go to sleep.

Nightmares, nightmares, nightmares.
I feel scared.

Nightmares, nightmares, nightmares.
He gives me a chase.

Nightmares, nightmares, nightmares.
My face is sweaty.

Nightmares, nightmares, nightmares.
I went to sleep.

Ashfaq Mohammed (11)
Sidney Stringer CTC School

Bullies

As I get onto the bus at 8.00am I see all the terrifying faces
looking and laughing at me
All of them joking and pulling faces at me.
It comes to my school stop I've survived the 2 mile journey
I reach out my trembling hand to press the stop-bell.
Being bullied for me is so much worse than living in hell.
I step off the bus and then, faster and faster I begin to walk.
I could hear the voices as they get nearer and nearer, they begin
to shout and murmur.
As I feel someone's icy-cold fingers tug against my head.
All I see is bright-red as I close my eyes and turn around I begin
to dread.
They broke my glasses and then I said that's it, I've had enough,
no more.
I could hear my heart thumping louder and louder.
As I shout and curse I see their faces start to change
Then a fearful frightened voice trembles and said please stay calm.
It was only a little joke, I never meant you no harm . . .

Symone Thomas (12)
Sidney Stringer CTC School

Witches

Once there was a witch
She was quite rich.
She likes to drink your blood
and she plays on mud.
She wears a pointed hat
and always cooks a bat.
She is a horrible old witch.

Once there was a witch.
She's got one little stitch.
She likes to eat you up
in one little gulp.
If you moan and you groan
she will never leave you alone.
She is a horrible old witch.

Farhana Choudhury (11)
Sidney Stringer CTC School

Rage

You scream and shout and curse and fight
'But you'll be alright because it doesn't last'
You cry and whine and cannot define,
the hatred you feel and menace you find
'but you'll be alright because it doesn't last'
You tear out your hair, oh what despair.
You battle for control but it swallows you whole
You know the chaos caused and want it to pass
'But you'll be all right because it doesn't last.'
You wallow in grief and anger and hatred,
    and cannot contain it,
    my life I will take it.
    The fear and the sorrow,
    there is no tomorrow
'But you'll be alright because it doesn't last'
The madness declines and your head it reminds,
that remorse is now called for and calmness is near
and love and humour and even some cheer,
can now shine a light through the dark and the drear
    the agony and spite.
And I am alright because it didn't last.

Helen Martin (16)
Sidney Stringer CTC School

SCHOOL

School, school, school, 123
When you get home it's
'Do your homework.'
Homework, homework, homework, boring.
Go to bed,
Get up early,
You never get time to yourself.
            School, school, school.
Lesson after lesson, after lesson.
            Work, work, work.
Detention, detention, 123
Then merits, merits - whipee, whipee.
Then nag, nag, nag.
Maths at the end of the day
Phew! Phew! How easy the lesson is.
            School what a *nightmare!*

Suzanna Govier (11)
Sidney Stringer CTC School

WITCHES

Once there was a witch,
her name was Mrs Twitch, even though
she was a witch, she liked playing football
on a football pitch,
Mrs Twitch's cat's name was little bitch
but everyone called her little titch.
Mrs Twitch's favourite player was Alen Boksic.
Little Titch's favourite team was Norwich
Mrs Twitch always went out with Alen Boksic.

Shahab Ali (11)
Sidney Stringer CTC School

Wouldn't It Be Good

Wouldn't it be good if it was me,
standing in the tunnel waiting,
waiting for the other team.
I would stand there then lead my team out.
We would win, I would score,
and then, then I would lift the cup

Wouldn't it be good if it was me
with the winning lottery ticket.
The ticket that had all six numbers.
It would be a double roll-over week.
And no one else would have a winning ticket.
I would go and collect the money then just
spend, spend, spend.

Wouldn't it be good if it was me
on the Concorde going twice
the speed of sound but so, so smooth.
I would be on my way to Barbados
I would be the envy of all my friends.
There I would stay for a month with my best friend
and no adults.

Wouldn't it be good if it was me
in a car on my way to the palace.
The palace where I would meet the Queen for my OBE
I would turn up and she would personally greet me
we would go and have tea together
then I would be presented with my OBE.

Chris Bryant (13)
Sidney Stringer CTC School

Ghost

I saw a ghost
eating toast
halfway up the lamppost
near the railway coast.
It was the way ghosts have a feast
he was a horrid old beast
he got some yeast
and said: it was the least.
He said it was a present
and I replied it is very pleasant
I was shocked
'cause I was locked.
Then someone knocked
I tried to open the door.
The ghost was poor
I felt sorry for him.
His name was Tim.

Aneesa Begum (11)
Sidney Stringer CTC School

About My Family

I like chocolate
I like crisps.
I like ice-cream
but my mum hates it.
I like my mum and I like my dad
I like my sister but I hate my brother
because he is too naughty.
The day before my birthday came
I was happy but when it came, I was ill.
But I got a birthday present
from my parents.

Alfa Noor (11)
Sidney Stringer CTC School

GREED - (WHAT IS IT?)

What is greed?
It is all around.
Perhaps greed is just a fact of life,
all it seems to bring me, is lots of trouble and strife.
Yet still we ask the question, 'What is greed?'

I know a man who's greedy, he lives all alone,
in a great big house in Chelsea,
he likes to call it home.
He will not spend a penny on anything at all,
and he never lets anyone in, when they come round to call.
He lives life like a hermit, but that is his greed.

How, you may ask, do I know such a man?
but how do you know, who I really am?
I, could be that man, or a lady fat and small,
it leads me to ask if we, know anyone at all.
Everyone is greedy, in their own little way,
I, do things out of greed, each and every day.
So when I ask what is greed, who can really know?
I guess it all comes down to the seeds our parents sow.
They are the ones who teach us, what is right and wrong,
they are the ones who feed us and make us big and strong.

My greed is different, to yours, hers, and his,
I suppose it depends on what you think it is.
My mother once told me, that 'Everyone is unique,'
and she was right of course because everybody is.

The question 'What is greed?'
is not totally justified,
the real question should be 'What is your greed,'
so, tell me, what is yours?

Kay Smith (16)
Sidney Stringer CTC School

WE DIDN'T MEAN ANYTHING BY IT

I'm walking to school,
arguing with my friend on the way,
half the way, I walked by myself.
I've just broken up with her.
There's some other girls behind me.
Laughing and joking and having a right good old time.
They started saying nasty things to me.
I just ignored them and started walking faster,
They ran after me, pushed me and grabbed my bag.
They started emptying my bag and I said, hey that's mine.
One of the girls said 'Yeah and what are you gonna do about it'
I had enough by then, so I turned round, booted her in the shin
and slapped her in the face,
The girls said we were only playing,
We didn't mean anything by it,
They all said sorry and then ran away,
I felt much better of myself,
Now they're my good friends.

Claire Sanders (11)
Sidney Stringer CTC School

MY DOG'S EATING HABITS

Once, I didn't mean to, but that was that.
I yawned lying in the sunshine
and accidentally I swallowed an ant.

I'd rather eat dog food or
last night's left-over chicken legs.
I'd rather have hot pepper
all over my scrambled egg.

Then I opened my mouth on a
sleepy day and accidentally closed
on an ant going that way.

It tasted kind of salty
it didn't throw a fit
it crunched down very nicely
and that was the end of it.

Vanisha Parekh (11)
Sidney Stringer CTC School

MATHS

First lesson in the morning
There goes the gong
I don't want to go
It'll be so long.
You there, say these numbers
I said it wrong
Oh my, it's 1 2 3 not ABC
Okay now try again
No sir, I've got a pain.
Okay new groups
You're in high, you're in low
No sir I don't want to go!
One more chance, say these
I hear the kids say easy peasey
Oh the numbers 1,2,3
The kids, I see them stare at me
Gong!
Yes! saved by the bell.

Puja Joshi (11)
Sidney Stringer CTC School

Sandwich

Sandwich, sandwich
Sandwich is great
Sandwich is nice
Sandwich is hot as spice
Sandwich is as cold as ice.

Sandwich, sandwich
Sandwich is made of
loaf of sliced bread
Sliced cheese
Spread with butter
Handful of lettuce
Sliced cucumber.

Sandwich, sandwich
I love sandwich
I could have a sandwich at breakfast
I could have a sandwich at lunch
I could have a sandwich at dinner
and any time and anywhere.

Amirah Sheikh (11)
Sidney Stringer CTC School

Islam

I was walking to the mosque
S suddenly I see the teachers go past
L oozing at them I knew I forgot something
A ll I remembered was I forgot some books.
M y mind flashed and said it's a dream.

Mohsin Jamal (11)
Sidney Stringer CTC School

Hiccups

Hiccups, hiccups, all day hiccups,
I get tired of my hiccups.
I get them when I am in class, I get them when I am in the bath.
I cannot walk, I cannot talk, because of my stupid hiccups.
My hiccups have now grown so old, my hiccups have now
grown all bold
I do not know what I will do,
But I am sure you will help me too,
If you do not know what I mean.
I will tell you what I mean,
I have been to the hospital, I have been to the doctors,
but they have no idea of what's got inside of me,
but it doesn't matter I will always live with them,
and they will always live with me.

Jameela Bhayat (12)
Sidney Stringer CTC School

The Dinosaur That Was Big And Bony

The dinosaur that was big and bony,
went to town and sat on Mr Stony.
Then it went and sat on Mr Hussain
who collapsed and said that he had a pain.
Then it went and sat on Mrs Kaurs who got scared
and ran indoors,
and last of all it went and sat on the clown
the poor clown died, Mr Stony cried,
'Don't cry I'm your friend.' said the dinosaur
who was big and bony.
So Mr Stony was very happy
So he changed the dinosaur's nappy.

Haroon Motas (11)
Sidney Stringer CTC School

SCORING AT WEMBLEY

I hope and pray,
that one day
I go and play
at Wembley,
for the gleam in my life
the smile on my face
that would be just ace.
To run out the tunnel
I know that would make mum proud.
To play up-front with Dublin for City,
would be a thrill,
and only if we could win one-nil
could you imagine the story
if we had the glory.
With Kieron Peacey doing the scoring.

Kieron Peacey (11)
Sidney Stringer CTC School

WHAT FRIGHTENED ME

Once when I woke up in the morning,
I was yawning and when I turned round
I saw a rat
I screamed, 'Trevor, *Where's my cricket bat!'*

But Trevor was snoring away
in his best T-shirt in memory of the D-day
I never knew what to do
so I picked up my shoe
and attacked the rat.
I whacked it!

The rat had his sudden death
it also had bad breath
so I threw it down the loo
and praised my *shoe!*

Sunny Seemar (11)
Sidney Stringer CTC School

DEATH

The tallest towers,
The darkest caves,
cannot keep it away.

Gates of iron,
Doors of steel,
cannot protect you from it.

Emperors of all time,
Kings of the world,
were not protected from it.

Guards and chains,
locks and bolts,
cannot hold it back.

For when it comes, it sweeps,
Taking who it wants,
Whenever it pleases,
No one can control it.

Tis death!

Sabiha Kathawala (16)
Sidney Stringer CTC School

My Hobbies

I like football
I like it very much
I also like tennis
but not quite as much.
The swimming I do at the baths
Is nothing more than a laugh.

Swimming, tennis, football, sport.
I like to be in my
Football shorts.

Tennis balls and
Tennis bats
It's up to you, to hit it back.

Football boots
and tennis bats
Balls and swimming hats
I like the sport and that's
for sure.
I also like my maths.

Singing, dancing
going mad.
Jumping round the room
Mike in one hand
Going B*oom! Boom! Boom.*

Chantelle Maconnachie (11)
Sidney Stringer CTC School

SEASONS

Winter's here for everyone,
so come on and join in with the fun.
Jumping, laughing, making snowmen,
and some people wish that winter wasn't here.
Summer is here, nice and hot,
playing out and having lots of fun,
going to the ice-cream man and asking for one,
taking it home and making sure it's all gone.
Spring is here and the flowers are blooming,
looking at them makes you all dizzy,
turning around and singing out loud.
Springtime is here.
Autumn is here and the leaves are falling,
leaves all lying on the ground.
When it's autumn, animals sleep,
and they don't say good morning till
autumn has gone.

Laura Monaghan (11)
Woodway Park School & Community College

UPSIDE DOWN

Upside down, around on the ground.
Inside and outside, spinning around.
The sky is bright, sometimes at night
up in the air spinning everywhere.
The trees are bright green
spinning at night giving everyone frights.
Dark nights, dark nights, give
everyone frights. Oh dark nights.

Kylie Cannon (11)
Woodway Park School & Community College

TEARS

With tears that fall,
a mother's name is called.

Heart beating hard and fast,
not knowing if the next would be the last.

White face and eyes open wide,
from the bullets I try to hide.

It's my tears that fall,
It's my mother's name that I call.

Not knowing for how long I have cried,
not knowing that in fact my mother has died.

Sophie Bodinnar (13)
Woodway Park School & Community College

ENGLAND V ITALY

Goal!
Wright's scored.
England cheer.
The crowd go wild
But Pearce fouls Zola.
The whistle blows.
Penalty,
Silence.
Goal!

Kirsten Kalns (12)
Woodway Park School & Community College

The Crash

The pilot's name was Billy McIver.
The people say he is a terrible driver.
He has crashed the plane 25 times
because he flies so low, and in squiggly lines.
It was a dark stormy night over the Atlantic
and the fuel went low, and the crew went frantic.
As it started to snow, they lost radio
and the engine spluttered and started to blow
Everyone screamed and shouted as they jumped out.
There was a big splash and bang as it hit the water
and that was the end of Mr McIver.

Robert Fellows (11)
Woodway Park School & Community College

The Vampire

The vampire awakes,
he flies silently through
the city.

He attends her room,
he bites her neck,
he sucks her blood
until she's dead.

He flies back to
his tomb,
and sleeps all day long.

'Blood,' he says.

Jane Kendrick (13)
Woodway Park School & Community College

Inside Of My Head!

In my head there
is a brain,
With tissue and
some veins.

Imagination creeps
and crawls
But reality
remains!

In my head there
is a skull
Pure white with
teeth and all.

Oxygen all around
going to my brain,
My nerves are going crazy
because this test we'll have on Spain!

Ann Wilkins (12)
Woodway Park School & Community College

My Mate And His Snake!

My mate was near his fate,
When he had a tangle with his snake.
They hissed, cried, fought and fought,
And guess who came out best,
The snake of course!

Kevin Warwick (12)
Woodway Park School & Community College

A Visit To Count Dracula

'Twas Hallowe'en night when the bats are in flight
And the ghosts rise to dance
By the moon's silver light.
Count Dracula woke
And opened one eye.
It's the day of my party!
Was his blood-curdling cry.

Meanwhile outside in a dark spooky place,
One guest, the werewolf,
Was combing his face and his chest and knees.
Then put on some powder
To get rid of the fleas.

The mummy was singing a tune from the Nile.
He's been ironing away for a very long while.
This suit is hard work
He angrily sighed.
It's a hundred feet long
And one centimetre wide.

One by one, through the night
Over mountain and moor
The howling guests met outside
Dracula's door.

Hearing their moans and his doorbell
Chime, he cried, they've arrived
And they're all dead on time!

David Chapman (13)
Woodway Park School & Community College

The Man Who Lost His Head

One afternoon, Bill realised he couldn't find his head.
'I know how you lost it,' his workmate Trevor said.
'You lost it when you laughed,' his friendly pal explained.
'I'll tell you just what happened. Remember when it rained
Early on today? We were drinking cups of tea
And Barney told a joke, you know about the Irish Sea?
Well anyway you liked it, and you really laughed a lot,
I thought that you'd fall over, but thank goodness you did not.
Instead your head went rolling and fell straight off your neck.
Poor old Bill, you laughed your head off.'
Said Bill, '*Well flipping heck!*'

Lisa Doyle (11)
Woodway Park School & Community College

The Witch

There is an old hag
Who carries a black cat in her bag
She lives on a hill
Where the sky is black
And always carries spells in a sack
The witch never talks
The witch never sings
She tries to do other things
Spells, cauldrons, worms and frogs
She turns people into logs
She puts them in the yard
And chops them all up
This is a wicked witch
Who always says 'Yuk!'

Beckie Derby (12)
Woodway Park School & Community College

SPIDERS

Spiders here,
Spiders there,
Spiders creeping everywhere.

I like spiders,
You might not.
My mother hates them too.
My brother said if I had a pet spider,
He'd squash it with his shoe.
I said to him that's not fair,
And he'd better beware,
Because he might find some in his bed,
Crawling everywhere.

Spiders here,
Spiders there,
Spiders crawling everywhere.

Jennifer Keen (12)
Woodway Park School & Community College

SPELLBOUND

All at night, quiet and calm
Apart from low chanting near
The farm.
Witches hover around the black
Cauldron making a spell for us to
Come.
The next morning people start to ask
Why is it *we* have to die, the witches
Reply 'Be quiet and get on with your
Task.'

Nicholas Stalham (12)
Woodway Park School & Community College

THE GOOD WITCH'S HOUSE

Inside it's bright,
And is just the right . . . size.

It's made from bricks and mortar,
And has running water.

Gardens front and rear,
And a chip shop near.

3 bedrooms I have,
Upstairs and downstairs there's a lav.

The kitchen is neat,
Where I make my lovely *big* treats.

There's a pond in the garden,
Flowers all around,

With a weeping willow stuck in the ground.

Thomas Allsopp (12)
Woodway Park School & Community College

GOING TO SCHOOL

Going to school, what did I see?
Loads of people staring at me.
I smiled, they turned away,
I was going to school today.

I was going through the gate
what did I see?
I saw some people climbing up a tree,
My face went blue, my face went white,
I almost lost my sight.

Lee Doughty (11)
Woodway Park School & Community College

In The Misty Glow Of Night

In the misty glow of night,
Three hags gaze into our fear,
For there lies the secrets of life,
That are forthcoming nearer to here.

They look into nature and every desire,
For they know what burns within the fire.
They can change the future but not the past,
They can alter time with the hour-glass.

They have a connection with everything,
And they know what it can bring.
They can make things grow from a tiny seed,
But they know within rising it will bleed.

They are forever rising into the light,
From the misty glow of night!

Anthony Agar (13)
Woodway Park School & Community College

Evil Spell

Venom of an adder snake,
Volcano's lava, earthquake's shake.
Thunder roars and rain storms.
Devil's fire and angel's choir.
Cats miaow, dogs bark,
Add a bit of scary dark.
Boil and sizzle in the pot
Until it's bubbling really hot!

Eleanor Morgan (12)
Woodway Park School & Community College

Down The Road, Next Door But One!

Down the road, next door but one,
There is a house covered in plums,
It really looks so nice and sweet,
We thought it would be a real big treat,
Until we found out what goes on,
Down the road, next door but one,
We hear them chanting every night,
It gives us all a real big fright,
They shout out, 'Bubble, sizzle in the pot
Make sure it is nice and hot,
Stir it, stir it, stir again,
Don't forget the heart of hen.
Add the innards and the toes,
The fingernails and the nose.'
It is a mystery to unfold,
It makes us shiver and go cold,
So there it is the hags have won,
Down the road, next door but one.

Kathryn Nickolls (12)
Woodway Park School & Community College

Food

Every day and every night
They jump out and give me a fright.
They grab an apple and an orange too.
Then they shout 'Food found'
They give me an awful fright
And then take a big fat juicy bite.
My brother likes sausages,
My sister likes hippopotamuses.

Lee French (11)
Woodway Park School & Community College

WALLACE AND GROMIT

Wallace and Gromit,
They work as a team -
To fly to the moon
And keep windows clean!

They had 'A Close Shave'
With Shaun the sheep.
Into the machine he went -
His wool came out in a heap!

With Wallace's quick thinking
And Gromit's machine -
They knitted Shaun a jumper,
With a stripe of green!

Flying off to the moon
Was always an ambition.
'A Grand Day Out' they had -
There was no competition!

On the moon they landed -
There was cheese galore.
They had a picnic,
On the cheesy floor!

Inventing is a hobby of Gromit's,
His next gadget could set alight!
'The Wrong Trousers' -
They didn't quite go right!

With Wallace in them -
Definitely out of control,
The penguin was there,
Taking him for a little stroll!

Jennifer Kenning (13)
Woodway Park School & Community College

We Heard

We heard a cackle upon the bridge,
We saw a fire burning bright
In the dark and misty night,
We heard chanting
            Double trouble, boil and bubble.

We heard the hags,
Chanting loudly, stirring quickly,
The cats miaowing,
The swoosh of the broomsticks as
            they glided through the sky,
The hags gave their cackle laugh
As they watched us shaking and shivering
They made me quiver with fright,
In the dark and misty night.

The hags started to chant
            Double trouble, boil and boil
As they faded in the dark and misty night.

Kelly Harper (12)
Woodway Park School & Community College

My Pets

My hamster bites,
And it hurts a lot.
His name is Scampy,
And to be cooked like one, he is not!

Charlie though is nice and gentle,
She is my pet fish.
We feed her fish flakes,
But not on a dish!

Sam's fish Tamagotchi,
Thinks he's the best.
But if it came to the challenge,
He'd never beat the rest!

But all my pets are lovely,
Swop them for the world, no can do!
And if any of them were to die,
I'll cry, boo, hoo, hoo!

Claire Flear (12)
Woodway Park School & Community College

The Vampire

He's asleep not making a sound.
Milk bottles filled with blood
but tonight's the night
it's time to scare
He wakes in anger
his stomach is rumbling
he tastes the air
licking his lips
He knows there are houses
nearby
He sees one
he is in the room
Makes a bite mark on her neck
He now leaves the room as
quiet as a mouse
He sneaks to his coffin
for another night's nap.

Rachael Clamp (12)
Woodway Park School & Community College

WITCHCRAFT

People get scared when demons are in sight
And also things that go bump in the night
So with a wizardy whoosh and a wizardy whee
I'm going to get some ingredients for me
So with an eye of a bat
And a tail of a cat
Now let me see how about that
Hmmm a little more spice would be nice
So I'll add something rather mad
Like something strange that's been eaten by dad
Or how about a rat
Regurgitated by a cat
Some of us witches like doing that
How about that let me have a taste
Eeurrgh! It tastes like bat dropping paste
Now how about a mouse or a gerbil
At least it's not anything herbal
Now it is perfect
I shall change my dialect
Now to put it to the test
Which customer do I think of best . . . you!

Carl Bonsor (12)
Woodway Park School & Community College

WITCHES

In the light of a fire three witches sat,
One, two, three and a cat.
On top of the flames, a big black pot,
Already the bottom flaming hot.
Inside was a witch's brew,
Looking like a terrible stew.
Eye of cow, leg of frog,
Tongue of horse, tail of dog.

One of the witches scratched her boil,
The cat's claws digging into the soil.
All this under the dark night sky,
While one witch got her broom to fly.
Now we leave the witches where they sat.
One, two, three and a cat.

Sam Smith (12)
Woodway Park School & Community College

FRIENDS

They're there when you want them, and sometimes when you don't
they do take no for an answer, but sometimes they won't.

They're loyal, they're good,
you treat them how you should.

They've got a certain style, they've got a certain way,
when you're feeling low, they're there to make your day.

They're kind, they're sharing,
almost all of the time, they're caring.

When you're feeling lonely, they're always there for you,
a good shoulder to lean on, a person to talk to.

They're sporting, they're fair,
they really do care.

Friends are brilliant, friends are great to you,
but when the day is over, remember, you're their friend too.

David King (12)
Woodway Park School & Community College

THE WITCH

The witch, the witch so very old
The witch, the witch creepy and cold

The witch, the witch scraggly clothes
The witch, the witch where she comes from nobody knows

The witch, the witch her skin so green
The witch, the witch so very mean

The witch, the witch all alone
The witch, the witch made of skin and bone

The witch, the witch squinting eyes
The witch, the witch small in size, but with the power to
close your eyes!

The witch, the witch so very old
The witch, the witch creepy and cold

The witch,
the witch,
the witch . . .

Darren Gray (12)
Woodway Park School & Community College

MY BEDROOM

My room is nice,
All painted Mexican spice.
Cosy as can be,
Dark and nice to see.

My room is fine,
The wardrobe, shelves, desk and drawers are pine.
I don't clean it much,
But my mum does as such.

Sun, moon and stars,
I can hear no cars.
Matching curtains and quilt,
So that's the way my bedroom is built.

Karen Leddy (12)
Woodway Park School & Community College

My Lovely 3-Course Meal

I had a three-course meal,
on the twenty fifth of May,
I wasn't very lucky,
to relive it the next day.

I won't go into detail, but,
there was cabbage in the toast.
The ice-cream full of vegetables,
a lovely, mashed up roast.

The revolting recipes' resurgence,
landed on my mum's bookshelf,
the carrots, caviar, gravy too,
I couldn't help myself.

Now please don't cry, or run away,
don't turn away in disgrace,
How do you think *I* felt,
when I saw it come from *my* face.

I hope we've learned a lesson,
from this poem of mine today,
don't fill up on three course meals,
chocolate's better *any* day.

Ryan Tyrrell (12)
Woodway Park School & Community College

I Hate School

I used to like PE,
I thought it was my cup of tea,
At football a good goal I scored
'It's the wrong end' the crowd all roared!

For science I had Mr Mo,
He said 'I'll show you the way to go'
But what I mixed was not quite right,
For it blew him right out of sight!

My maths teacher thinks I am a fool.
'What is 3 x 8?'
'32' I said after a long wait
'32? Whatever shall we do with you?'

Steven Law (12)
Woodway Park School & Community College

My Dream About Ice-Cream And Two Plants

Roses are red
Trees are green
I like ice-cream

I had a dream
about an ice-cream
If you like ice-cream
you will be in my dream
about an ice-cream.

So think of a dream
about a lovely ice-cream
with green ice-cream and red roses
in your big and lovely ice-cream.

Jane Bottomley (12)
Woodway Park School & Community College

THERE'S A SPIDER IN MY BEDROOM!

There's a spider in my bedroom
It's really big and hairy
It crawls about at night
And it's really scary
I try to squash it with a shoe
But I'm too scared to go anywhere near it.

There's a spider in my bedroom
It's really big and hairy
One day it crawled upon my hand,
And it was as light as a fairy.

There was a spider in my bedroom
It was big and hairy
But now there's nothing left of it,
Because it's dead and buried!

Emma Harper (12)
Woodway Park School & Community College

MY BROTHER

My brother is very mad. He jumps around
like my dad.
When I've tidied my bedroom. He makes
a mess.
So when I'm not there and he messes it up.
I go spare and then I turn into a bear.
It's all so quiet in the middle of the night.
He starts crying and it gives me a fright.
But he's only three and I know he loves me.

Ben Taylor (11)
Woodway Park School & Community College

Snow!

Gently falls the cold white snow,
It trickles down my nose.
It's freezing cold but I'm not bothered,
'Cos I can't feel my toes.

I call my friends, they come around,
We have a snowball fight.
We make an igloo out of ice
But what can we use for a light?

We build a big tall snowman,
With a carrot as a nose.
Then we used stones for his smile,
His eyes and his toes.

Now the fun is over,
We've no more time to play,
But don't be sad, it's actually quite good,
'Cos tomorrow's a brand new day.

Kerry Goodchild (12)
Woodway Park School & Community College

Witch Recipes

Yellow thick custard,
Mouldy apple pies,
All mixed together with,
Dead dogs' eyes.

Bucketfulls of vomit,
Big slimy snails,
All mixed together with,
Pigs' curly tails.

Fresh hot water,
Little dragonflies,
All mixed together with,
Birds from the skies.

Bottles of bleach,
Slugs that leave trails,
All mixed together with,
Fresh toenails.

Samantha Evans (12)
Woodway Park School & Community College

FRIENDS

I like my friends even when
they:
    Poke and prod
    Pinch and snitch
    Tell tales
    Start fights
    Annoy me
    Punch me
    and just get on my
nerves!
    But what I can't stand
    is them doing
    it all at
    once

Aarrgghh!

'Help me please, Miss!'

Paul Rule (11)
Woodway Park School & Community College

Hallowe'en

Out amongst the night so dark,
The witches made their scary start.

Spooky spells were all around.
Throwing insects on the ground.

'Twas the night of Hallowe'en.
Ghosts and ghouls were everywhere to be seen.

Pointed hats and long finger nails.
Witches' black cats with long furry tails.

Suddenly night time turned to day
And all the witches flew away.

Helina O'Brien (12)
Woodway Park School & Community College

Missing Them

I'm missing them, I'm missing them,
What can I do?
I wish that they were here,
What can I do?
They are gone, they are gone,
What can I do?
I need them, I need them,
To help me get through.

If only they were here,
If only they were here,
I wouldn't be missing them,
If they were here.

Megan Davies (11)
Woodway Park School & Community College

WITCHES AND WIZARDS

Witches and wizards,
Boiling a brew,
Bat's wing, dried lizard,
Watch out they're after you!

Wizards and witches,
Run and scream,
They'll hide in ditches,
This is no dream!

Flying on a broomstick,
Chasing boys and girls,
Give them a kick,
Then watch the witches hurl!

Wizards can be sneaky,
Witches can be too,
Make sure your floors are creaky,
Or they'll sneak up on you!

There's magic in their fingers,
They'll turn you into frogs,
Their horrible odour lingers,
Quick, let loose the dogs!

It's even worse at night,
They'll magically appear,
They'll give you such a fright,
And make you run in fear!

Martyn Hall (12)
Woodway Park School & Community College

My Letter

They might call Old Trafford
The theatre of dreams,
Because it shines in the sun
Sparkles and gleams.

Fifty five thousand supporters
Will crowd, they'll sing noisy songs
And chant very loud.

The players arrive
In their smart black suits,
And head for the changing rooms
To put on their boots.

They might have millions
To throw around,
To buy new players
And build a new ground.

But all of these things
That I've put in my letter,
Coventry City
Can do ten times better.

Gemma McLean (12)
Woodway Park School & Community College

My Brother

There once was my brother called Pete
Who captured a whole fishing fleet
He said 'Don't be scared,
All your lives will be spared
I only want something to
eat!'

Michelle Batley (11)
Woodway Park School & Community College

My Brother

My little brother Billy
looks just like Mrs Tilly.

He is ten and
he loves my ink pen.

He loves to walk
but does not talk.

He is skinny and
acts like little Jimmy.

He is quite bad
and hates my step-dad.

My brother Billy looks like
my uncle Jimmy.

He is quite dim
but I must love him.

Lynn Magee (12)
Woodway Park School & Community College

Snow

S now
N o one around
O ver the ground
W inter has come
B ushes covered in snow
A nimals sleeping
L ong cold winter is here
L ong cold nights around
S now is around.

Victoria Holmes (11)
Woodway Park School & Community College

My Family

I have two brothers and one sister,
Aaron, Rebecca and Christopher.

Christopher is seventeen,
Aaron is five.

Rebecca and me are in between,
Rebecca is fifteen.

I am Emily,
and I am eleven.

And mum's due,
to have a baby.

I live with mum and Paul,
Chris lives with dad.

Rebecca and Aaron,
live with us too.

I share a
bedroom with Rebecca.

Aaron has one to himself,
Isn't he a lucky chap.

Emily-Jane Anderton (11)
Woodway Park School & Community College

We Can't Wait!

We can't wait to criticise,
We can't wait to tell lies.
We can't wait to watch him cry, as he denies.
We just can't wait.

David Saunders (11)
Woodway Park School & Community College

The Chimpanzee

When I looked in the mirror
I thought I saw a
Chimpanzee.
I didn't think it looked like me,
but the big brown thing spoke to me.
The chimpanzee made a roar then
he began to
snore.
'Are you angry?' I said, then he nodded
his big brown head.
'What is the matter with you, chimpanzee?
Have you got a swollen
knee?'
'No, no,' he said, 'I have got a
thumping head.'

Michelle Pollock (11)
Woodway Park School & Community College

My Family

What can I say about my family?
I love them loads and they love me.

My dad goes out to work all day,
My sister always gets her own way.

My mum is in the house all day,
She cooks and cleans, never time to play.

My dogs are called Pippa and Titch,
Pippa acts normal, Titch acts like a witch.

All the same I love my family,
Because they make me really happy!

Kimberley Accardi (11)
Woodway Park School & Community College

LIFE

Why do we live?
Why do we die?
Why do we cry?
And why do we lie?
These things I will never know until I
go!

When I go how will I know
if there is a place above?
If there is a heaven or a God?
And if he controls us all?
And will I walk down a long long hall
until I get to a wall
where the gates will be opened for us all?

I don't know the answer to
any of these things.
Even though I'm good at technology
and writing anthologies.

Life is one big puzzle, you never
know what you're going to guzzle.
Also I will never understand why
we live on land?

Oh why? Oh why? Oh why?

Katie Greer (11)
Woodway Park School & Community College

My Family

My dad is very weird
He hasn't got a beard.
He is sometimes very funny
And he has quite a lot of money.

I love my mum a lot
She has got a cot.
Ready for the baby
But she is a nice lady.

I have two sisters who are pains
And they like riding on trains.
We sometimes have silly fights
But they both have very hard bites!

I have a step-dad as well
Which no one can tell.
My mum and Steve had been married
for nearly a year.
But he never cries, I have never seen a tear.

My family are very nice
And we all like egg fried rice.
Even though there is not ten
You still have to love them.

Paul Stower (11)
Woodway Park School & Community College

THE CAT AND THE BUNNY

This poem is about a little cat and bunny.
They both decided that they were very short
of money.
They checked their wallets hopefully, they could
not find a bean.
They realise that they had wiped their
wallets clean!
They went upstairs to go to sleep,
But all they could do was give a sorrowful weep.
'I'll go to the bank' said Bunny with a tear
in his eye.
But I am not going on my own, I'm far too shy!'
The next day came, they went to the bank.
When they got there, their little hearts sank.
The bank manager said 'You're badly in debt
Get out of my bank or I'm calling the vet!'
On the way home they found five pound.
They jumped up and down on the ground.
'Yes, we're saved, we have some money.
Let's go to the shops' said eager Bunny.
They bought some milk and sweeties too,
and some toilet roll for their loo.
They went upstairs to their beds
and being tired nearly dropped dead.
'Goodnight,' they mumbled to each other and
went to sleep and oh yes, they did not weep.

Keely Walker (11)
Woodway Park School & Community College

BASKETBALL

Some people like dunking biscuits,
But I've got news for you,
I like dunking basketballs,
That's the thing I do.

You need to be really tall to make
Basketball your game
For if you have long arms and legs
It will really help your aim.

This is it, my team will work
We are hoping we shall win,
But now the opposition has the ball.
Our chances are looking slim.

The ball rebounds, it's in my hands,
Now it's my turn to shine.
I turn around to take my aim
That basket's finally *mine!*

The team we are playing are top of the league.
We know they are the best.
But at the end of the day,
If we win,
We'll be better than the rest.

Adam Harper (11)
Woodway Park School & Community College

Life

Life is good, sometimes bad
Life can be happy or sometimes sad.
Life is about saving others' lives,
You may get hurt by a beehive.
Life is something you cannot ignore,
Watch your life you won't get one more.
Life is about *peace* and *love*,
One of the most lovely birds is a dove.
Life is about caring for others, being generous
and happy. At the start of your life you have
to wear a nappy.
Life is about you and other people too!
Life is about happiness and joy.
You may be a happy girl or boy.

Emma Porter (11)
Woodway Park School & Community College

My Sister!

My baby sister dribbles,
All down her pretty bib,
Although she's a lot of trouble,
She always looks cute in her crib.

She likes to play
With Squeaky, Spaghetti and Piggly
Although she's got no teeth or hair
Her toes are kind of wiggly.

Kayleigh Martinez (11)
Woodway Park School & Community College

What If?

What if the world were flat you see,
Where would people including me, be?
What if we were up in space
and did not carry on the human race?
What if the sky all caved in one day
Where would we all be
and where would we stay?
What if we hadn't come to earth
and the sea wasn't here so we couldn't surf?
What if? What if? What if?
I've always wondered all these things
Why does the dashing bluebird sing
So sweetly up in the tree, oh why
Oh why, oh why, can this be?
So I've answered all the questions in one
Put them in a poem
and said what is to be done.
You can work these all out for yourself
What if? What if? What if?
Maybe there just isn't an answer
Anything could be the right way
So I'd thought I'd say, these last few words
What if? What if? What if?

Sarah Watkins (12)
Woodway Park School & Community College

The Birthday Bash

Today it is my birthday.
I woke up very early
To find no presents at all.

I decided to go to school.
I was as early as a teacher.

Everyone at school just acted
Like it was a normal day.
Everyone at school went home
at twenty past three.

When I got home there,
Was no-one to be seen.

One step through the door,
There was a jolly song.
There were cakes and lots of presents.

Steven Leeming (12)
Woodway Park School & Community College

Why Is The Sea So Blue

Why is the sea so blue?
How do we know if it's true,
When the sky is blue and the grass is green
but why is sea so blue?

It twinkles at night with the help of the
stars,
If you look closely you might just see Mars.

Danielle Wells (11)
Woodway Park School & Community College

FOOD

Food, food, oh food, food, food,
How would we live, without our food?
Chocs give me spots,
But sprouts keep me healthy,
I eat lots of sweets really doubtfully!
Some like chicken, some like fish,
Some eat theirs in a dish.
I love food
(Couldn't live without it)
Some hate food,
(But I really doubt it!)

So take my advice,
And don't be silly,
'Don't waste food and be a dilly!'

Jodi Eales (11)
Woodway Park School & Community College

HEDGEHOGS

I like hedgehogs.
They like me.
I like hedgehogs when they look at me.
They are cute
But not very clean,
I like hedgehogs, it doesn't bother me.

Even though I don't see many,
I don't think we should be cruel to any,
They have numerous spikes
And more than one flea.
I like hedgehogs it doesn't bother me.

Jason Bull (12)
Woodway Park School & Community College

My Brother

My brother Sam
Is a pain in the neck
He's always running around.

He jumps up and down
Like a mad old clown
And moans when he doesn't get his way.

He plays football
But I think he's sad
Because he thinks he should be the best.

At the table
He isn't able
To say a word without a burb.

That's why he's my brother Sam.

Mark Bennett (12)
Woodway Park School & Community College

Paradise

Long sandy beaches, warm air,
Cool sea, palm trees, where?
Paradise! That's where.

Beautiful place of mine,
Enjoying, passing away the time,
Oh! Beautiful place of mine.

So cool refreshing sea,
Waves splashing against me,
Keeping me cool from the sun,
While I swim having fun.

Green glorious mountains,
Surround this beauty.
The scent of pine wafting in the air.
How I longed, again, to be there.
My beautiful paradise Mauritius.

Charlotte Gluyas (11)
Woodway Park School & Community College

I Wish I Had A Sister

I wish I had a sister
I really, really do
I would be so happy
I would feel glad too.

I wish I had a sister
We might not get along
I would borrow her clothes
And make-up too
If only I had a sister.

I would have someone to
Talk to.
We could talk about boyfriends
If only I had a sister.

Jade Griffiths (11)
Woodway Park School & Community College